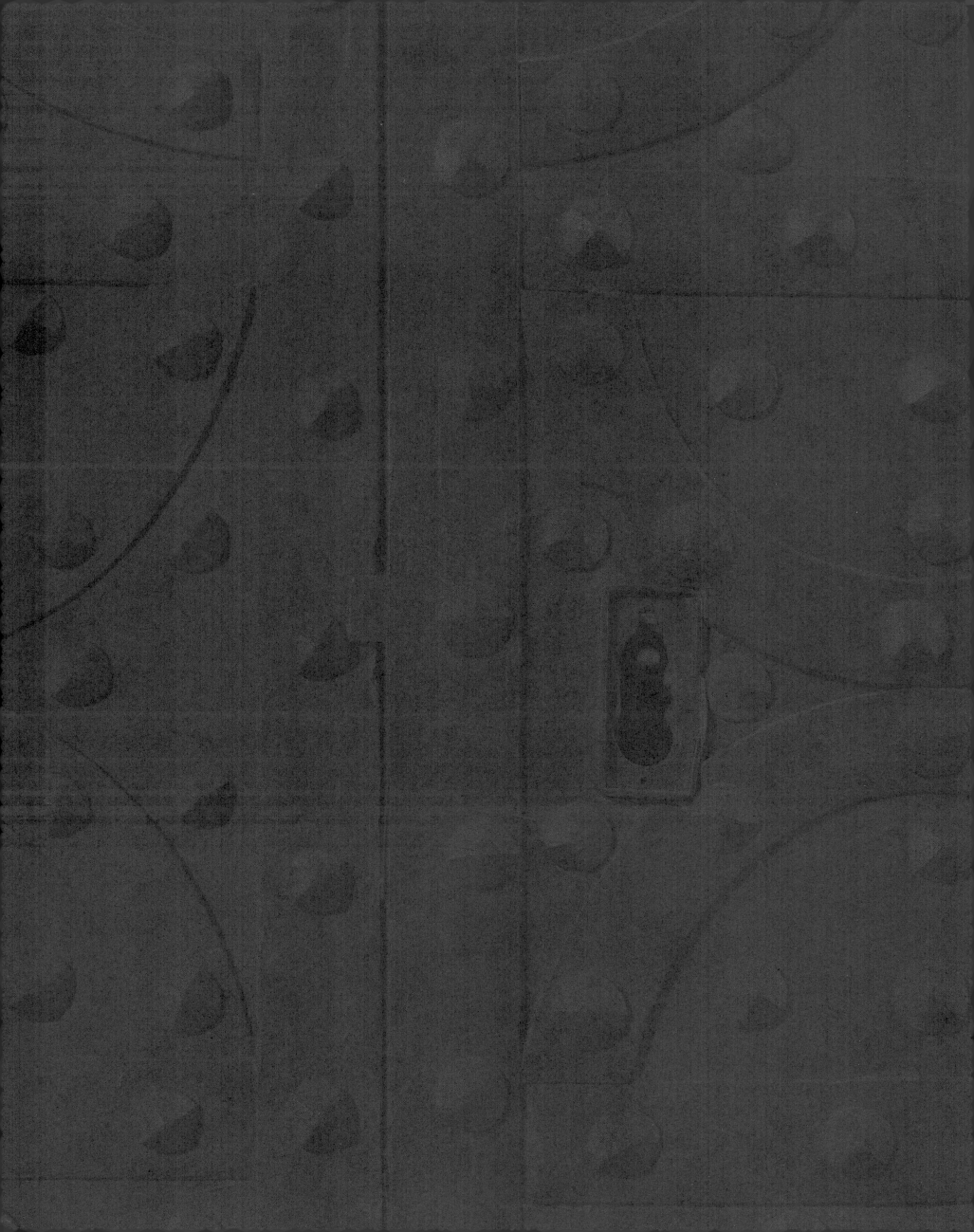

Beauty & Mischief
The Design Alchemy of Blackman Cruz

Adam Blackman & David Cruz, *with* Stacie Stukin
Foreword by Ryan Murphy
Book design by Iain R. Morris

Mennonite petticoat upholstered fauteuil
on front cover by Clarke & Reilly

CAMERON + COMPANY
Petaluma, California

Contents

Foreword by Ryan Murphy
8

Introduction
10

Chapter 1 • THE GOODS
25

Chapter 2 • TURN-ONS
119

Chapter 3 • HABITATS
175

Chapter 4 • BLACKMAN CRUZ WORKSHOP
225

Chapter 5 • COMRADES
265

Epilogue
282

Afterword
284

Thank You & Gracias
286

Bibliography
287

Colophon
288

Foreword

I moved to Los Angeles in the late 1980s with one piece of furniture I shipped from Washington, DC—a love seat. From Ikea. It was teal.

This raises the question: Can style be taught? Probably not. Some things are ingrained. But I think you can be mentored in this arena. I certainly was—by Adam Blackman and David Cruz, the proprietors of one of my favorite stores in the world.

My first visit to their showroom, nearly thirty years ago, was a crash course not just in style and décor, but in history. Their curiosity was infectious. I vividly remember Adam patiently leading me around and answering all my questions. And there were many. David would later do the same.

These partners in crime have very different styles, but that is the joy of their store. In the Blackman Cruz world, everything is an exuberant mix. Their wondrous eye taught me how to furnish an interior. My first purchase was a doozy I couldn't afford at the time, but I bought it anyway—a 1940s Italian chair upholstered in chartreuse linen.

The most indelible lesson that Blackman Cruz—both the store and the men—taught me is that authentic taste should be a combination of styles and things you love. Not everything has to match. The best interiors thrive on this tension. Most people have been indoctrinated by magazines and tastemakers that argue that one style must dominate. Blackman Cruz proves the opposite. The joy and the fun of living comes from mixing styles, obsessions, and interests.

Their store reflects this philosophy. Furniture from all decades, handmade objects, and found treasures small and grand live harmoniously on their showroom floor, imparting a vision: This is the way to live. The space is so relaxed and livable that you can invite a group of people to the shop and host a marvelous dinner party.

Blackman Cruz is now part of my history and the first place I visit when I furnish a home. It's personal—my three children have grown up around objects and furniture that Adam and David seemingly curated just for me. The beauty, oddity, and specialness of these items have launched many family conversations.

Over the years, I have purchased an array of fantastic and fantastical objets d'art. I designed a whole room around a pair of gigantic caryatid goddesses from the 1860s. On a gray winter day browse, I discovered stained-glass lights fashioned by hand in the shape of skyscrapers by Adam Kurtzman, who is now one of my favorite artists. A pair of iguana-shaped brass and enamel door handles by the Mexican designer Pepe Mendoza; an ebonized nineteenth-century table in the form of Pan, the Greek deity who was a companion to nymphs; and a plaster bust of Barbra Streisand—these are some of the reasons I keep coming back.

The Babs bust is probably my favorite. It holds court at the entryway of my Provincetown house, and I'm always thrilled my childhood idol welcomes visitors to my home.

Blackman Cruz is and always has been one of the best places not just in Los Angeles, but in the entire world. Their passion informs and inspires anyone and everyone who is lucky enough to wander into their wonderful showroom, as I did decades ago.

—Ryan Murphy

Introduction

It's delightfully apropos, given the combination of drama and play that infuses the sensibility of antique dealers Adam Blackman and David Cruz, that their Highland Avenue showroom is part of Hollywood's louche cultural history. The space, previously occupied by Probe, one of the most famous gay discos in America, was immortalized in Paul Schrader's iconic film *American Gigolo*, where an Armani-clad Richard Gere navigates the dark, mysterious hallways in search of his pimp. Probe defined an era of community and rebellion, fantasy, and intrigue, an ephemeral moment with enormous impact.

When Blackman Cruz acquired the building in 2007, the disco ball was long gone. All that was left were old booze bottles, ashtrays with cigarette butts, a few matchbooks, and memories, like the time Chaka Khan allegedly drove her Excalibur into the front of the building. In collaboration with architect Allen Kolkowitz, they reimagined the space as a container to hold their eccentricities. They opened the floor plan into another type of Hollywood dream stage where they could create environments, tell stories, and allow clients to time travel. Within a few steps, one can go from 1930s Paris to pre-Columbian Mesoamerica to 1950s Italy, while learning something new about the history of decorative art and beauty. Along the way, you're likely to stumble upon some mischief, like a pair of French nineteenth-century mirrored brothel chairs or a sculptural display of antique barbells.

These diverse portals into other worlds are by design and happenstance, the result of two men with different interests and points of view coming together to share the same space. They have been called an odd couple, and while they are not life partners, they are business partners who thrive on the friction and harmony that drives their dichotomy. Blackman has an affinity for the quirky and quintessential—a pair of chairs from Al Capone's Wisconsin retreat called the Hideout or a passion for Richard Blow's postwar Montici pietra dura plaques. Cruz's more classical predilections, rooted in his Mexican heritage, show up in a rare 1930s Arturo Pani desk or in the fine metal styling of a baroque Sicilian gilded mirror.

Cruz came to Los Angeles from Chihuahua, Mexico, and unhappily toiled as an advertising art director until he figured out how to turn his passion for travel, history, and shopping into a vocation. Blackman grew up in New Jersey and got his start in theater. When gifted a trove of Victorian clothing for costumes, he recognized a market for these rarities, opening the door to the intoxicating world of buying and selling at auction. The two met when they each had stalls at an antique collective. Eventually, they found a space on La Cienega Boulevard, and in that small West Hollywood showroom, they built a community of artisans, designers, and clients who admired their panache. They were known for Friday night speakeasies at the shop, audacious window displays, and an appreciation of industrial and macabre objects like mug shots, coffin carts, and embalming slabs, balanced by Jean Prouvé pieces or rarities like a pair of Frank Lloyd Wright andirons.

When Blackman Cruz opened their doors in 1993, the established dealers in the neighborhood who bartered in traditional antiques referred to them as "the junk store on the corner." Undaunted, they carried on, trailblazing a model where one shop could display a varied selection of American and European furniture and objects including contemporary works, as well as hero pieces from centuries earlier and varied cultures.

In time, they earned respect for their learned approach; a confident, idiosyncratic style; and their commitment to assembling a worthy collection of what they call "life enhancers," designed to do just that: enhance quality of life. They attracted art-world professionals, architects, celebrities, and top-tier interior designers, many of whom came up in the industry along with them.

This freedom to let the eye wander toward what piques curiosity is a luxury Los Angeles affords. It's a town where traditional Georgian, Tudor, Craftsman, art deco, and Mediterranean style homes coexist with international, avant-garde stylists like Paul László, Rudolph Schindler, and Richard Neutra. Later case study architects like Pierre Koenig and those who democratized good design, like A. Quincy Jones, helped solidify a Los Angeles modernism that ushered in John Lautner's expressionism. Glamorous designers to the stars such as Billy Haines and maximalists like Tony Duquette added another layer to the legacy of a city that's often characterized as not having a center.

But to understand Los Angeles, one must realize it's a whole comprised of parts influenced by its immigrants, past and present, and the industries of this imperfect metropolis. Blackman Cruz embraces all these influences, creating a visual language that literally takes you globe-trotting into an aesthetic that's guided by instinct and sometimes serendipity.

Beauty & Mischief explores this vision. It's not an exacting science, but rather a respite from the computer age that encourages you to slow down and enjoy the luxurious warmth of a patina that washes away the noise of modern life. Hopefully, in these pages, you'll discover your own inspiration outside the dictates of trends and find the conviction to know, as the ever-confident interior designer Dorothy Draper once said, "If it looks right, it is right."

This book, which celebrates a thirty-year career, will also highlight a little history about some of their favorite decorative artists. Blackman and Cruz will take you into their homes in Los Angeles, Ojai, and San Miguel de Allende. You'll see a survey of the customized pieces created in the Blackman Cruz Workshop (BCW) and read profiles about some of the talented artisans they represent.

The Blackman Cruz ethos runs the gamut, from operatic to telenovela. This frisson between eras and generations allows for unexpected twists and turns, which are rarely perfect. But admit it: Perfect is boring, visually and in life. Embracing this alchemy of beauty and mischief liberates Blackman Cruz to forge a design identity that fosters surprise and delight. British raconteur Quentin Crisp's quote, featured on the invitation to their opening, best sums it up: "It's no good running a pig farm badly for thirty years while saying, 'Really, I was meant to be a ballet dancer.' By that time, pigs are your style."

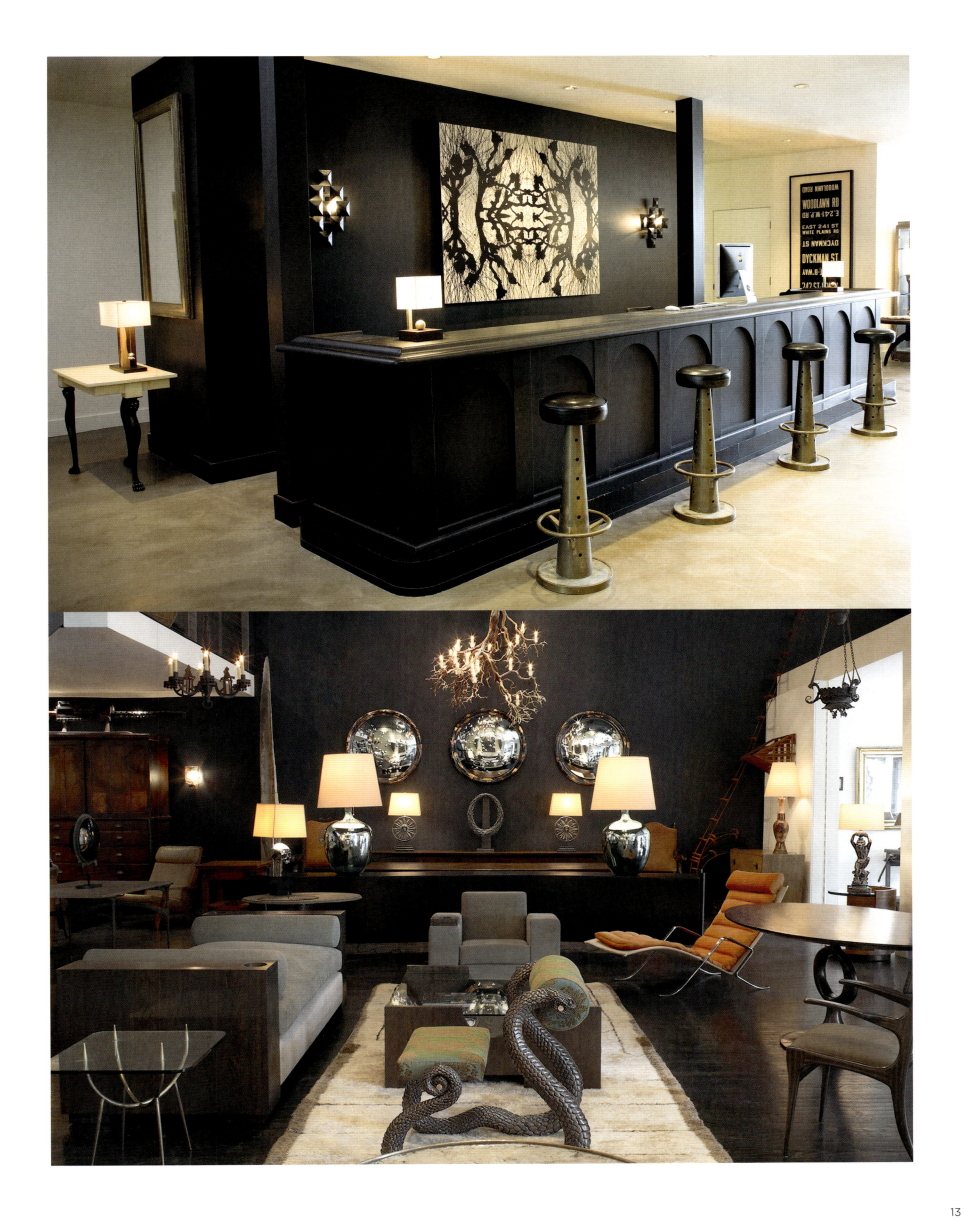

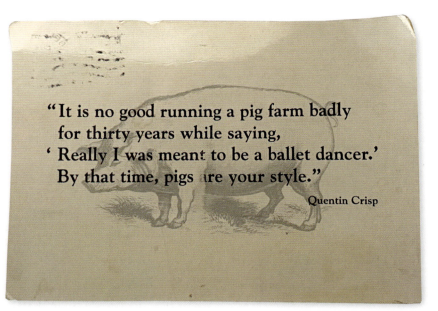

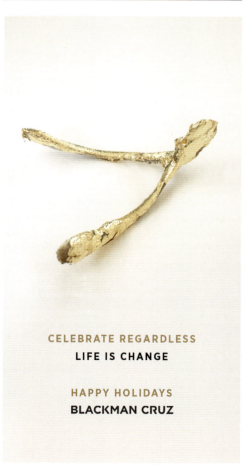
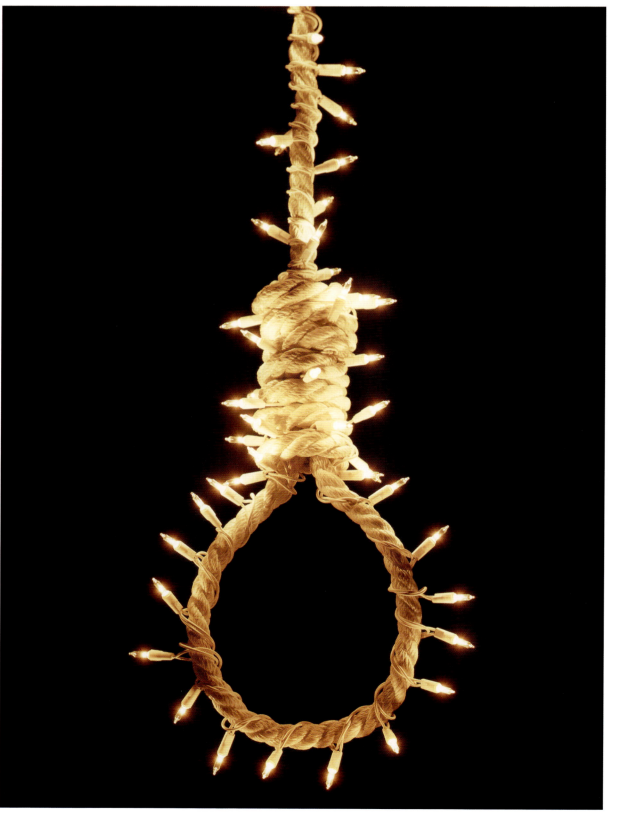

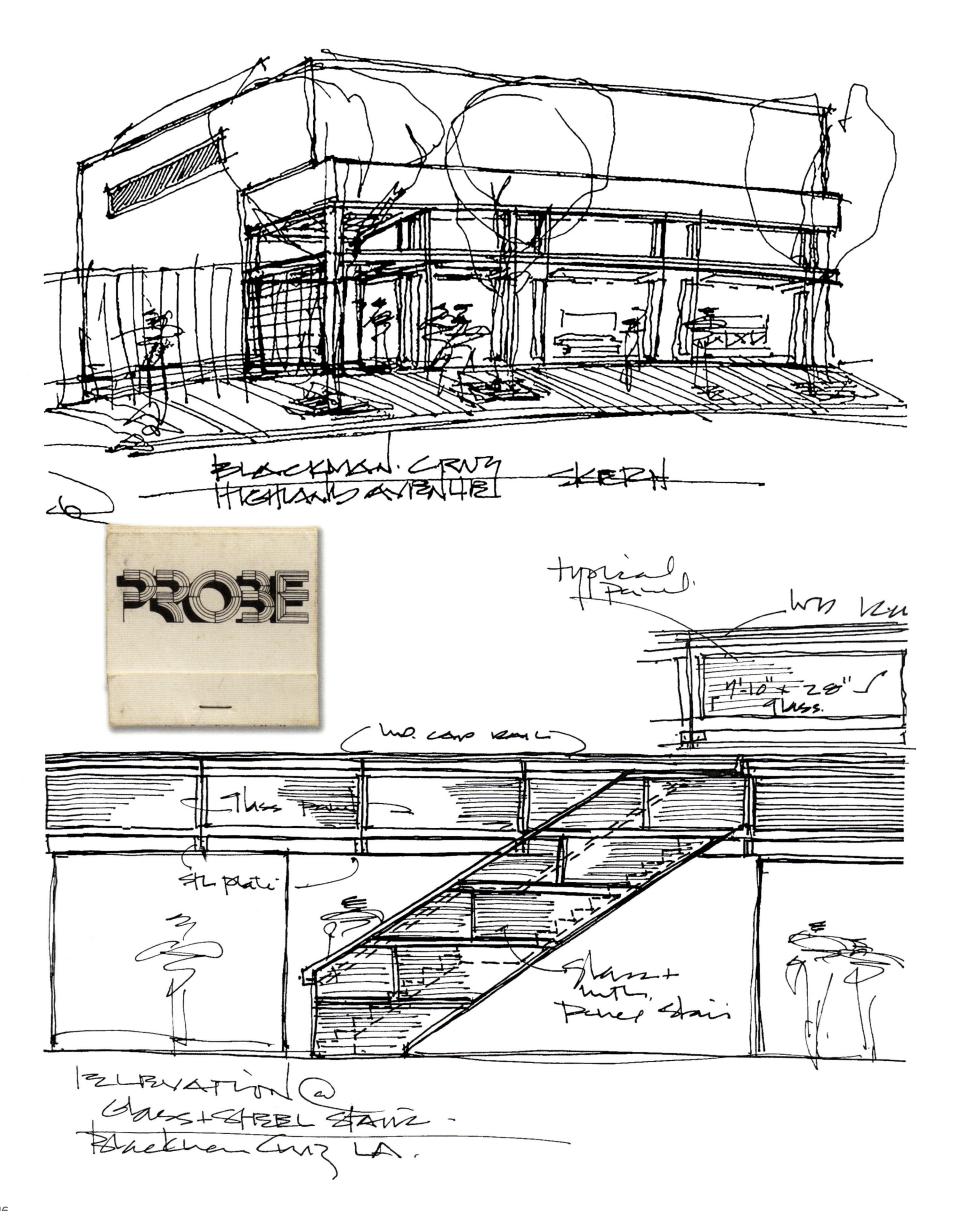

PAGE 1
TOP TO BOTTOM: *Nineteenth-century Victorian bell jar with wax fruit; live snake; Blackman Cruz Workshop (BCW) Deliquescent Table*

PAGES 2–3
LEFT TO RIGHT: *Four-panel eighteenth-century chinoiserie screen; BCW Deliquescent Table; organic root vessel; Japanese ikebana usubata; creamware pitcher; pair of eighteenth-century finials; gilded tabletop vanity mirror; BCW Boudoir Brass Ball Series Lamp*

PAGES 4–5
LEFT TO RIGHT: *Antique leather box; rustic work table, ca. 1880; framed nineteenth-century burka; collection of BCW Brutalist Prickets; eighteenth-century leather and iron sheepdog collar*

PAGE 6
CLOCKWISE FROM TOP LEFT: *BCW 3-Squared Sconce in nickel; Vittorio Introini P700 Shelving Unit from the Proposal Series; BCW Op Table in nickel; Peruvian eighteenth-century majolica urn*

FOREWORD
PAGE 9
Ebonized Pan center table, England, ca. 1860

INTRODUCTION
PAGE 10
Inscribed Polaroid of Adam and David, taken by Annie Leibovitz during a visit to the showroom

PAGE 11
Clock face from the Stewart-Warner Factory, 1905

PAGE 12
TOP: *Lika Moore, Adam Blackman, and David Cruz*

PAGE 13
TOP, LEFT TO RIGHT: *BCW Athena Writing Table; BCW Brass Ball Series Two-Way Table Lamp by Lika Moore; brass-framed mirror; BCW 3-Squared Sconce in nickel; BCW Brass Ball Series Wenge Boudoir Table Lamp by Lika Moore; abstract photo; BCW Yacht Stools; New York subway destination sign* • BOTTOM, CLOCKWISE FROM TOP CENTER: *BCW Constellation Mirrors; custom tree-branch chandelier by Lika Moore (made as a gift for Adam and Kate Blackman's wedding); bronze memorial garland; pair of bronze sun medallion lamps; pair of oversized Mexican mercury-glass table lamps; Fabricius & Kastholm FK 87 Grasshopper chaise lounge; BCW Op Table; BCW Neoclassic Armchair; BCW Snake Chair; BCW Screening Room Coffee Table; BCW Screening Room Club Chair; BCW Pierced Side Table; BCW Screening Room Day Bed; BCW Skull Table Lamp in nickel*

PAGE 14
TOP: *Opening party invitation* • MIDDLE & BOTTOM LEFT: *Holiday card designs by Jeff Price* • BOTTOM RIGHT: *Holiday gallows card from 2008: "Celebrate Regardless"—humor in the face of a collapsed economy*

PAGE 15
TOP: *Holiday card: "Happy Holidays, Baby" with red painted plastic dolls; 1950s Italian parchment and brass dining table* • BOTTOM: *Halloween window display with artist Adam Kurtzman's papier-mâché devil*

PAGE 16
TOP & BOTTOM: *Sketches by Allen Kolkowitz, architect* • MIDDLE: *Matchbook from Probe, the notorious private nightclub in LA from 1978–1999 and former occupant of 836 North Highland Avenue*

PAGE 17
Blackman Cruz's showroom under construction, with 1970s disco ball from LA's Club Vertigo

PAGES 18–19
CLOCKWISE FROM TOP LEFT: *Pair of Mike Diaz Coimbra mirrors; painted Italian armoire, ca. 1800; floral arrangement by Louesa Roebuck; pair of Mike Diaz Tripoli consoles; pair of Mike Diaz Sabudia Daybeds; Mike Diaz Gino Coffee Table; BCW Brutalist Prickets; Pepe Mendoza pedestal side table*

PAGES 20–21
CLOCKWISE FROM LEFT: *Pair of BCW Triball Lamps; leather wingback club chair; terra-cotta bust of Louis XIV; Dan Johnson Gazelle dining set; bronze urn; architectural fragment lamps; collection of glass vases courtesy of Lianne Gold; pair of BCW Small Studded Table Lamps; vintage infinity mirror; twentieth-century modernist horse-head sculpture; Dan Johnson coffee table; Thonet bentwood rocking chaise lounge; modern console table*

PAGE 22
CLOCKWISE FROM TOP LEFT: *BCW Constellation Mirror; mounted glass lens; pair of Max Ingrand for Fontana Arte sconces; collection of nineteenth-century charcoal studies; BCW Elephant Ear Wingback Chair and Ottoman; BCW Bronze Thebes Stool; Arturo Pani coffee table; BCW Deliquescent Table*

Chapter 1

THE GOODS

"You can't have everything. Where would you put it?" —Steven Wright

There's a recognition when you see an object, a chemical reaction in the primal part of the brain that instructs: Bring it back to the cave. It's like a romance. You see them across a crowded room, you must have them, and then the dance begins.

For Blackman Cruz, that waltz can be interpretive or deliberate. Since they don't specialize in niche styles or pursue formulaic trends, they're freethinking generalists who pick pieces they want to live with. After thirty years on the hunt, they've seen a lot, giving clients the benefit of trained eyes that focus on what intrigues. They're drawn to objects with histories that open doors into cultures near and far, from eras long gone or from the recent past, all revealing the hand of artists and craftspeople who put their spirit into a creation.

Blackman and Cruz work independently, gathering a mix of the curious and the refined. Blackman treks across the United States and abroad (he still loves a good flea market), stoking his passion to discover things he's never seen before. Like an early nineteenth-century ceremonial paddle from the Austral Islands in French Polynesia meticulously carved with a shark-tooth tool or the surprising rustic minimalism of French Alps château décor, where tree-trunk slabs were fashioned into rough-hewn cabinets.

Cruz stalks Mexico and Europe, with annual pilgrimages to the Parma Antique Fair in Italy, and trusted dealers who cater to his classical, expressionistic tastes. He might come home with a pair of Poliarte brutalist sconces that have a gothic tinge, or something esoteric, like a big architectural buffet designed by occultist Rudolf Steiner, whose theories on education, agriculture, and spirituality favor an organic style in which right angles are verboten.

The hunt is not always glamorous. It can be a dirty, dusty adventure that requires social wrangling for exclusive access, and predawn wake-ups with flashlights to roam antique fairs. Some pieces need to be rescued and require rehabilitation in preparation for their close-up. There can be miscalculations, like many years ago when a hole had to be cut in the ceiling of their first showroom to accommodate a fourteen-foot commercial clock face Blackman rescued from the 1905 Stewart-Warner Factory in Chicago.

In the early days, humble beginnings forced creativity. When they acquired a few turn-of-the century painted industrial metal cabinets from Europe, they stripped away the paint, leaving the unadorned steel finish. When they discovered similar, well-priced industrial pieces domestically, they bought those, adding medical display cabinets, articulated wall lights, drafting tables, daybeds, and even steel Windsor chairs. Recontextualized into domestic settings, these pieces, with their sturdy lines, sparked enthusiastic sales, and by the time Blackman Cruz moved on from the industrial, they had launched a trend replicated by retailers like Pottery Barn and Restoration Hardware.

Back then, before Google and Los Angeles's explosive gentrification, fortuitous discovery was possible, like the day Cruz walked by an antique store in the Silver Lake neighborhood of Los Angeles and saw a chair that looked like a butterfly. It was strange, a little ugly, but sometimes that eccentricity is the sweetest nectar. Upon closer examination, he discovered it was from the 1920s, signed by elite French furniture maker and interior designer Armand-Albert Rateau.

Today, that Silver Lake antique shop is closed, and Blackman Cruz has evolved, allowing for bolder moves. Recently, they acquired two enormous aluminum-clad crocodile lights designed in 1983 by Frank Gehry for Rebecca's, a restaurant in Venice, California. Created before Gehry became a world-class architect imprinting Los Angeles with his curvy, robust buildings, these rare examples of his sculptural artwork hung from the ceiling of the eatery frequented by his artist friends like Ed Moses, Sam Francis, and David Hockney. This time, installation didn't require holes cut into any ceilings. The twenty-one-foot mother and seventeen-foot child reptiles hang auspiciously above the furnishings in their Highland Avenue showroom.

For Blackman Cruz, ingenuity and instinct still drive the hunt. Taking a pair of turn-of-the-twentieth-century Mexican limestone property markers and reimagining these architectural ruins as garden sculptures appeals more than buying pedigree decorative arts with a stroke of the keyboard. That's not to say Blackman Cruz doesn't continue to acquire important pieces by designers like Clara Porset, Maria Pergay, Paul T. Frankl, Billy Haines, Josef Hoffmann, and Walter Gropius, to name a few. But they're often asked if there's anything new to find, and they will always answer yes. They embark on their quest with a tabula rasa mindset, untainted by judgment and preconceived notions, because that's the thrill of the hunt.

33

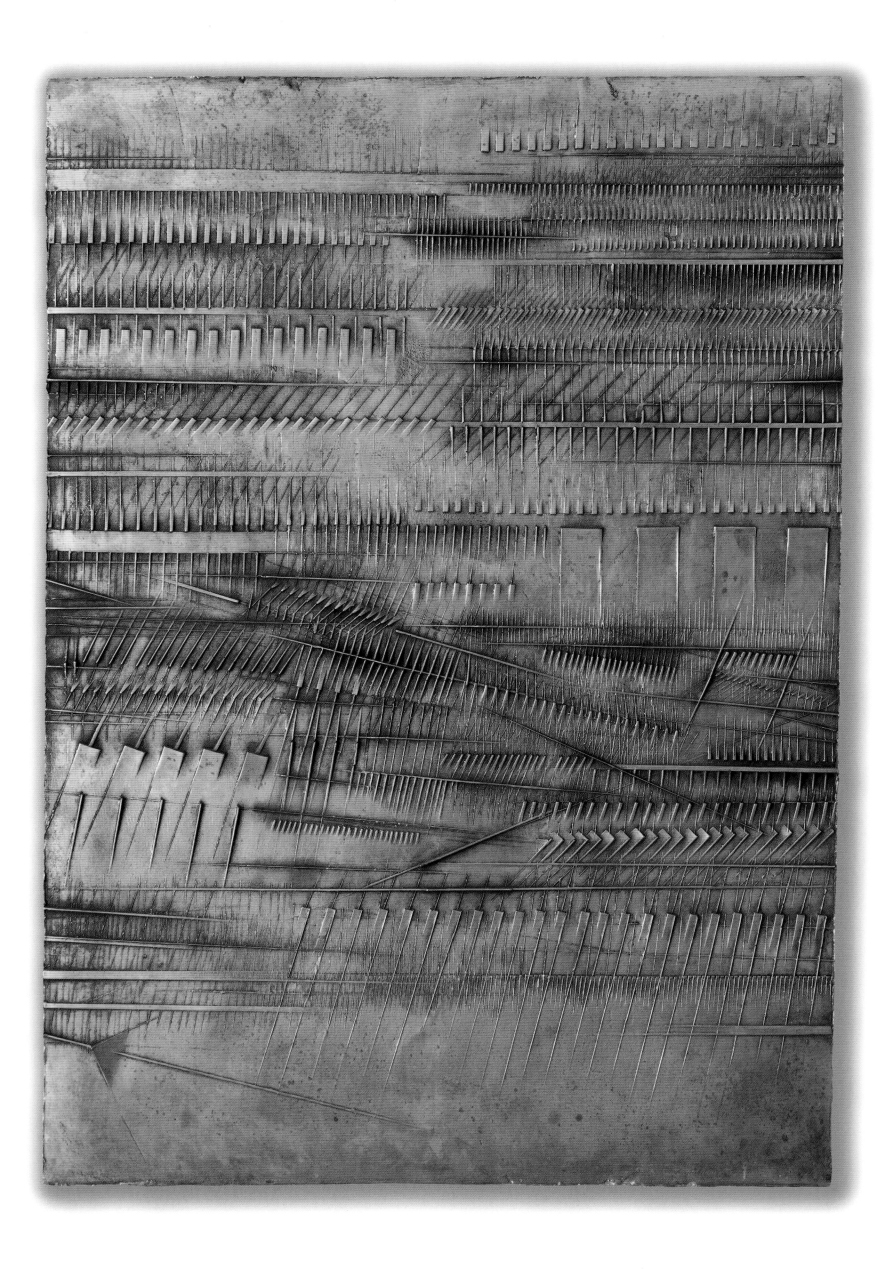

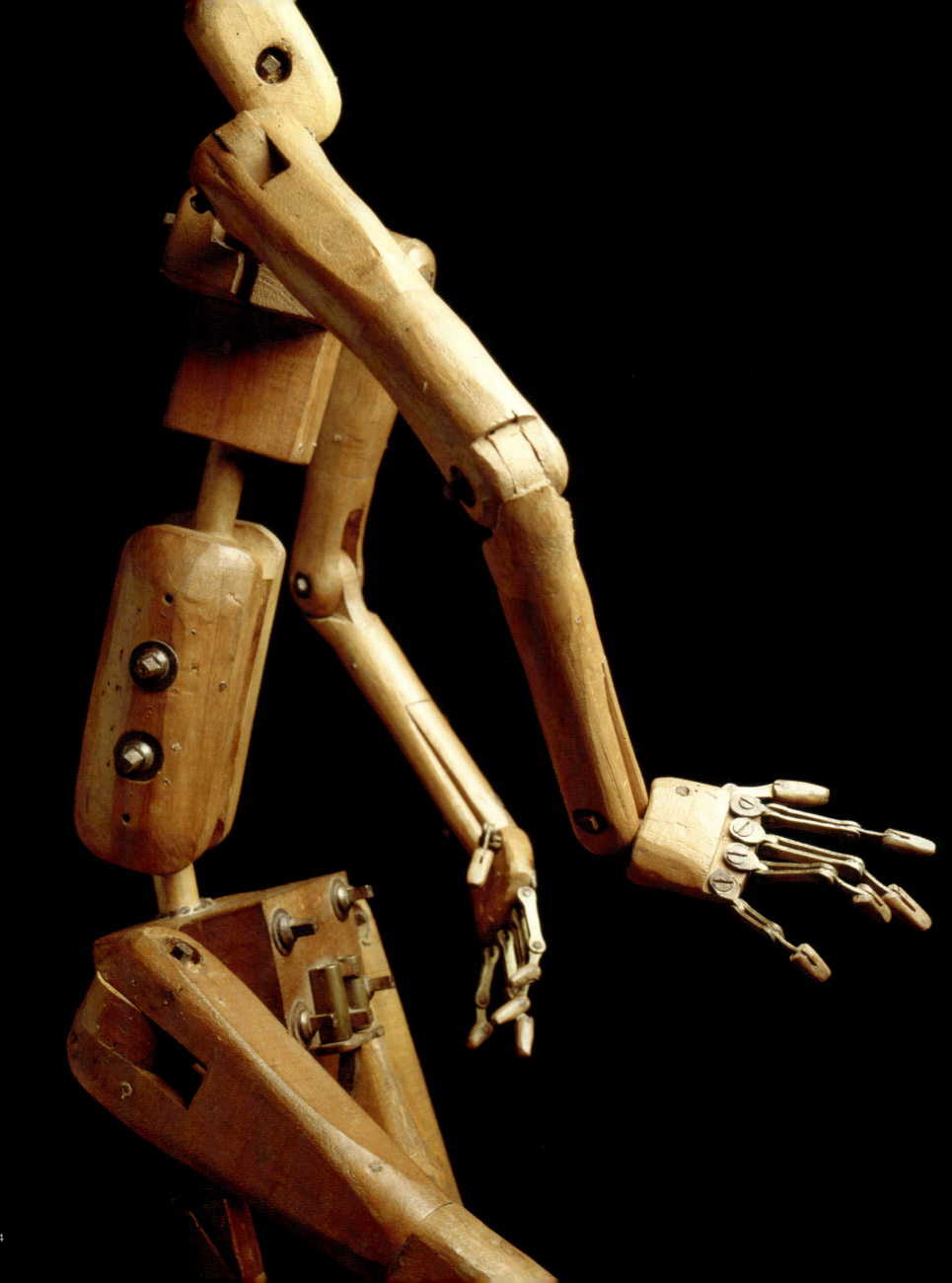

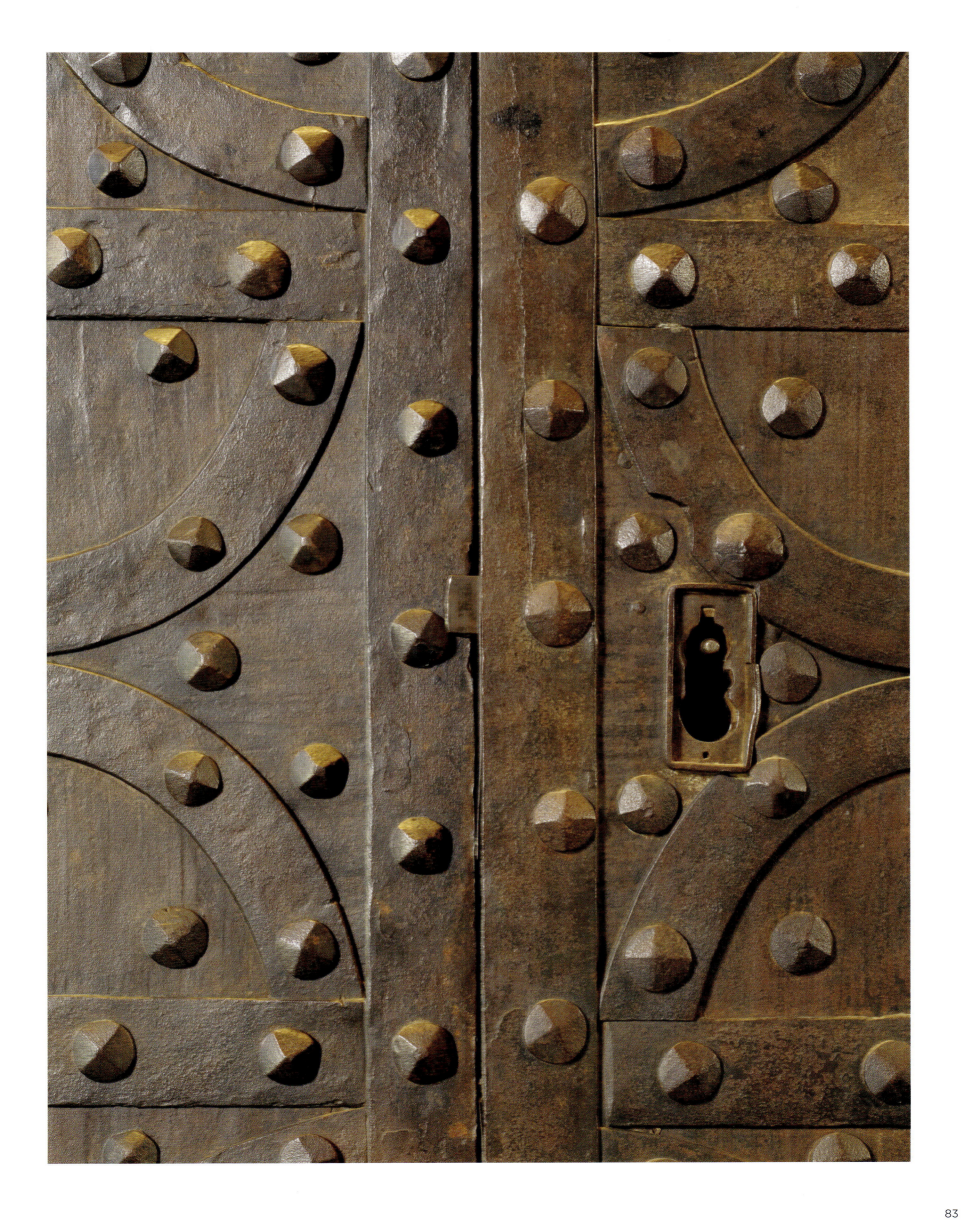

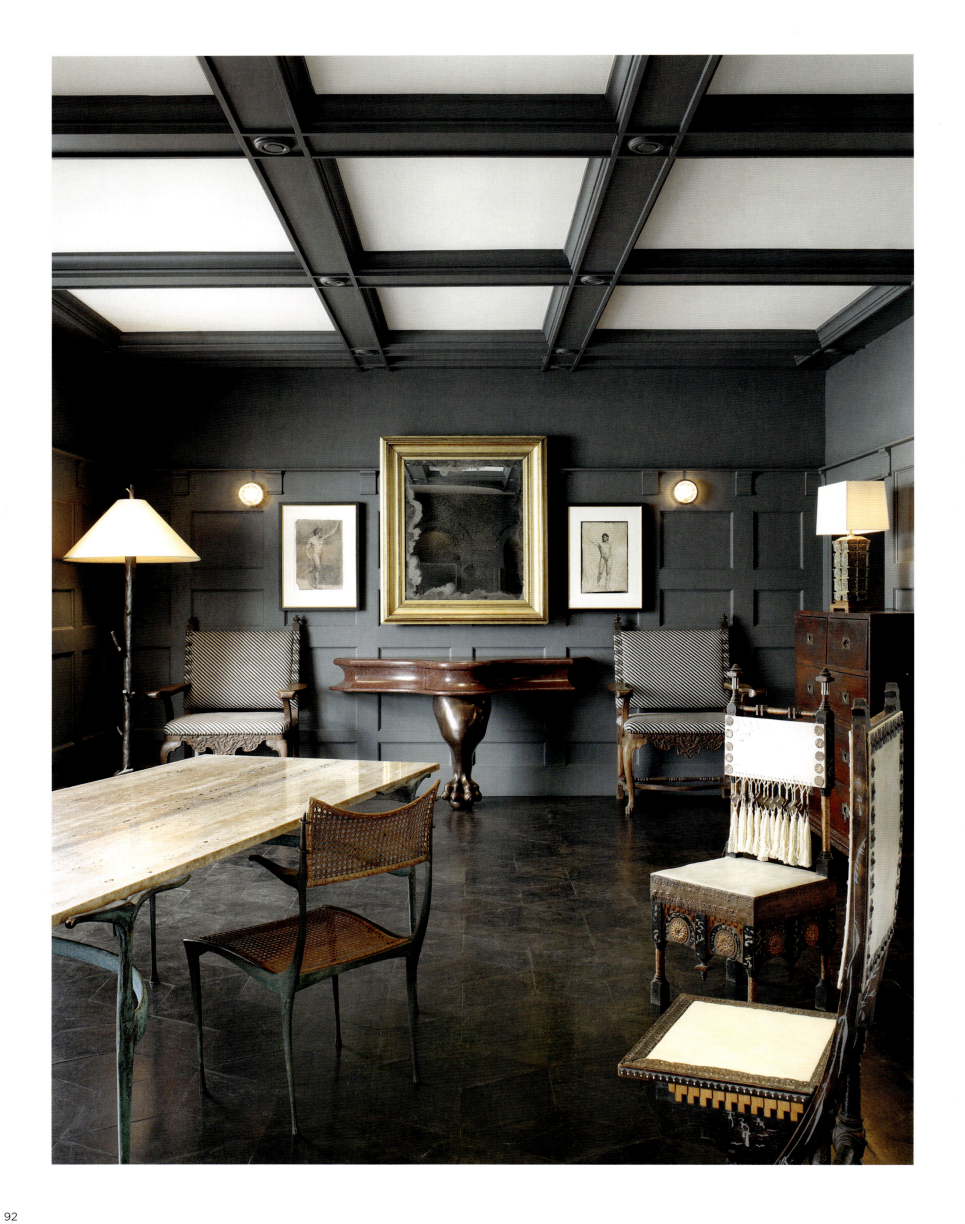

PAGE 27
Pre–79 CE Pompeiian marble and bronze sundial

PAGE 28
TOP TO BOTTOM: *Pair of French wingback leather patchwork lounge chairs, ca. 1975; Maison Jansen (attributed) yacht stools, ca. 1935*

PAGE 29
Raymond McGrath floor lamp, United Kingdom, ca. 1929

PAGE 30
Eighteenth-century Italian Santo fragment

PAGE 31
Model holding Grand Tour carved marble foot; Dan Pollock wood table

PAGE 32
Unique Italian copper and perforated glass coffee table, 1950s

PAGE 33
TOP TO BOTTOM: *Beaubourg stacking chairs for the Centre Pompidou; Edwardian tufted leather and nickel-plated iron chaise*

PAGES 34–35
TOP TO BOTTOM: *Collection of early twentieth-century carnival masks; wood library table with iron tusk tenon joints commissioned by Henrik Tati Schlubach, ca. 1945*

PAGE 36
Crown of thorns tramp art wall mirror

PAGE 37
TOP: *Monumental eighteenth-century Sicilian gilded metal frame with original mirror: This spectacular mirror springs right out of a Visconti movie.* • LEFT TO RIGHT: *Pair of Tulip Chairs by Fabricius & Kastholm; seventeenth-century Italian writing table; Roman marble headless bust on Mexican colonial wood plinth*

PAGE 38
Two twentieth-century abstract bronze sculptures

PAGE 39
TOP TO BOTTOM: *Detail; Archimede Seguso coffee table, ca. 1950*

PAGES 40–41
TOP TO BOTTOM: *Pair of Thierry Jeannot Ikal Sconces; model lying on a de Sede sectional sofa, 1970s*

PAGE 42
Cronaca 5: Paolo Gastaldi *by Arnaldo Pomodoro (b. 1926), bronze, etched "Arnaldo Pomodoro" and numbered 1/3, 1976*

PAGE 43
TOP TO BOTTOM: *Nineteenth-century Sicilian water-gilded tempietto; BCW bronze cast of pre-Columbian shell*

PAGE 44
TOP TO BOTTOM: *Chinese carved and decorated panel; stone-carved sculptures in the manner of H. R. Giger; eighteenth-century Italian chest*

PAGE 45
Sphinx *by David Edstrom (1873–1938), Sweden, granite, 1914: For almost three decades,* Sphinx, *which originally exhibited at the 1915 Panama-Pacific Exposition, was tucked away in a private collection and was thus published as "whereabouts unknown."*

PAGES 46–47
Collection of one hundred early twentieth-century framed vintage mug shots entitled 100 Guys Your Mother Warned You About: *Mug shots have been described as being a kind of photo booth for the American underbelly.*

PAGES 48–49
Pair of chairs from Al Capone's Wisconsin retreat, the Hideout, ca. 1920

PAGE 50
Maquette of nineteenth-century architectural staircase

PAGE 51
TOP TO BOTTOM: *Collection of seven continental wall mirrors; eighteenth-century Neapolitan dolphin fragment; three eighteenth-century Venetian carved-wood mermaid consoles*

PAGE 52
Pair of mirrored nineteenth-century brothel chairs photographed at Dana Hollister's spectacular Paramour Estate

PAGE 53
Late-seventeenth to early-eighteenth-century Italian armoire

PAGE 54
Monumental urn from Tonala, Mexico, ca. 1940

PAGE 55
TOP TO BOTTOM: *John Smith mosaic mural for the Petroleum Club, Statler Hotel, Los Angeles, 1952; José Luis Venegas Martinez unfinished-wood jacaranda sculpture; Dan Johnson Gazelle dining set, 1955; American glazed terra-cotta urn; Bauer oil jar*

PAGES 56–57
Karin van Leyden (1906–1977) and Paul László (1900–1993) custom four-panel screen from the estate of Barbara Stanwyck, 1947

PAGE 58
TOP LEFT (LEFT TO RIGHT): *Early twentieth-century carved stone satyr herm with nymph; gilded mirror; pair of frosted glass deco table lamps, 1920s* • TOP RIGHT (LEFT TO RIGHT): *enormous geodes; pair of Mexican terra-cotta finials* • BOTTOM LEFT (TOP TO BOTTOM): *Neapolitan grand tour bronze chair, ca. 1820; French sculpting stand* • BOTTOM RIGHT: *Carved basalt parrot with cactus, Mexico, ca. 1920*

PAGE 59
CLOCKWISE FROM TOP LEFT: *Large gilded wood framed mirror; mounted faux narwhal tusk; BCW Drip Coffee Table prototype; Clarke & Reilly sofa*

PAGES 60–61
LEFT TO RIGHT: Seagull *chair and ottoman by Gösta Berg & Stenerik Eriksson, Denmark, 1968; enormous sewer pipe wood mold; Dan Johnson* Gazelle *coffee table, ca. 1955*

PAGE 62
Fragrant *by Jeff Price (1954–2019), fiberglass and dirt, twenty-first century*

PAGE 63
CLOCKWISE FROM TOP LEFT: *Machinist table lamp; carved-bone balancing toy; radar tube in original shipping crate; two carved antique trophies; woven African metal hat; Noh theatre wood mask; eighteenth-century carved-wood finial; Italian walnut table*

PAGE 64
French life-size articulated artist's figure, ca. 1850

PAGE 65
Circus ball

PAGE 66
Detail collection of imperfect plates by Taller Experimental de Cerámica, ca. 1980

PAGE 67
CENTER: *Our production manager's dog and store mascot, Hudson, showed up for work every morning, rain or shine, treat or no treat.* • TOP TO BOTTOM: *Collection of imperfect plates by Taller Experimental de Cerámica, ca. 1980; nineteenth-century Northern European leather lounge chair*

PAGE 68
Victorian tufted-and-fringed leather wingback lounge chair

PAGE 69
TOP TO BOTTOM: *Collection of carved stone cartouches, ca. 1905; Gary Chapman centaur and satyr marionettes; nineteenth-century Italian walnut armchair*

PAGES 70–71
CLOCKWISE FROM TOP LEFT: *Pair of Italian 1920s Murano glass sconces; octagonal Italian painted framed mirror; pair of Mike Diaz Patria candlesticks; eighteenth-century Italian walnut and pressed leather sofa; carved-wood talon leg side table, ca. 1880; José Luis Venegas Martinez sculpture*

PAGE 72
TOP, CLOCKWISE FROM TOP LEFT: *Pair of BCW Brass Ball Series Two-Way Table Lamps by Lika Moore; terra-cotta bust of Louis XIV; BCW Screening Room Daybed* • BOTTOM, LEFT TO RIGHT: *Early nineteenth-century hand-stitched Nomadic tent panel; Mexican nineteenth-century bench with mythical eagle and snake carving on cactus, which is the Mexican national emblem*

PAGE 73
Twentieth-century 36-inch-diameter disco ball

PAGE 74
Brutalist pottery vessel by Stephen Freeman, 1990s

PAGE 75
Early-twentieth-century carnival mask of pig

PAGE 76
Tree of life table lamp, ca. 1910

PAGE 77
Guillotine cigar cutter, ca. 1910

PAGES 78–79
CLOCKWISE FROM TOP LEFT: *Pepe Mendoza table lamp; ornate lantern, ca. 1800, reinterpreted by Clarke & Reilly, 2005; Ernesto Tamariz bronze grasshopper, Mexico, 1956; pair of eighteenth-century Swedish washstands; pair of armchairs reinterpreted by Clarke & Reilly, 2005; twentieth-century Moroccan hand-woven wool rug; BCW occasional marble table; Chesterfield sofa, ca. 1870, reinterpreted by Clarke & Reilly, 2005; Danish coffee table, 1977, reinterpreted by Clarke & Reilly, 2006; pair of nineteenth-century Mexican animas figures*

PAGE 80
TOP LEFT: *Eighteenth-century Italian mirror, collection of pre-Columbian shells; Roman torso* • BOTTOM LEFT: *Pair of carved stone gothic architectural finials*

PAGE 81
Detail of monumental caryatid figure, 1860s

PAGES 82–83
Eighteenth-century Italian iron studded safe; detail

PAGES 84–85
Clarke & Reilly sofa upholstered with antique hand-embroidered manton de Manila

PAGES 86–87
1970s French bronze table lamp; detail

PAGE 88
TOP TO BOTTOM: Mike Diaz Potosi pentagonal mirror; monumental nineteenth-century mercury sphere; Mexican baroque polychromed stand

PAGE 89
Pair of Christine Delorie table lamps, ca. 1945

PAGE 90
Intricately carved eighteenth-century coco de mer with prayer for prosperity

PAGE 91
James Prestini, #255, nickel-plated steel sculpture, ca. 1970

PAGE 92
LEFT TO RIGHT: Dan Johnson dining table and chair; BCW Endangered Series Floor Lamp; pair of Spanish nineteenth-century upholstered armchairs; pair of cast glass Italian sconces; nineteenth-century charcoal sketches; BCW Leonine Wall Console by Lika Moore with a faux porphyry top; two Carlo Bugatti side chairs; English campaign chest, bronze Orientalist table lamp

PAGE 93
TOP TO BOTTOM: Japanese two-panel carp screen; pair of BCW Cone Lamps; Japanese bronze vessel; French desk, 1940s

PAGE 94
BCW Pompeiian Wind Chimes sculpted by Adam Kurtzman

PAGE 95
TOP: Collection of nineteenth- and twentieth-century dog collars • BOTTOM: Collection of iron barbells on stand, ca. 1910

PAGES 96–97
Italian mid-twentieth-century buffet

PAGE 98
Japanese root armchair and Japanese root stand, nineteenth century

PAGE 99
TOP: Ernesto Tamariz grasshopper bronze sculpture, Mexico, 1956 • BOTTOM: Eighteenth-century Neapolitan dolphin fragment

PAGE 100
French aluminum spiral staircase, 1960s

PAGE 101
Collection of Pierre Cardin Espace wrist watches, 1970s

PAGE 102
Anglo-Indian carved padouk camel occasional table, ca. 1900

PAGE 103
TOP: 1930s carved basalt jaguar exhibited at Carole Decombe's Viva La Vida show in Paris, 2018 • BOTTOM: Pair of carved-wood Escuela de Talle Directa y Escultura armchairs, Mexico, ca. 1930

PAGES 104–105
Pair of carved-wood Escuela de Talla Directa y Escultura armchairs, ca. 1930

PAGE 106
Japanese mythological figure, Edo period

PAGE 107
Seventeenth-century German fruit-wood marquetry table cabinet

PAGES 108–109
Pair of Paul Frankl custom leather swivel armchairs with ottoman, ca. 1948

PAGES 110–111
LEFT TO RIGHT: Chuck Moffitt match-type sculptures; Human Suitcase, by Richard Wheeler, twentieth century

PAGE 112
Pair of fraternal carved-wood throne chairs, ca. 1900

PAGE 113
Detail of continental nineteenth-century carved-wood sphinx

PAGE 114
LEFT TO RIGHT: Pair of eighteenth-century Italian hall benches; Videl multifaceted mirrors by Mike Diaz; Persian rug

Chapter 2

TURN-ONS

"The only way to get rid of temptation is to yield to it." —Oscar Wilde

There are discoveries that transform hunting and gathering antiques from a quest into a compulsion—that somewhere out in the world, whether it be Mexico, Europe, or the United States, there are more to be had. The designers highlighted here have become personal darlings and an important part of the Blackman and Cruz oeuvre, championed because their pieces are serious, unique, and sometimes have a bit of levity, creating enticing contradictions.

The earthy otherworldliness of Carlo Bugatti, the joyfulness of a pair of Pepe Mendoza sunburst lamps, or the indisputable glamour of Arturo Pani—these creators have a definitive voice that's a bit eccentric and unexpected, making them a touchstone of Blackman Cruz's alchemy. Blackman's zeal for automatons is about the animals, yes, but more importantly, it represents a historic period when innovation spawned an industry that was entertaining and novel. The awe and excitement of antiquities and religious iconography humbly remind us that our time on earth might be finite, but what we leave behind will inspire others in the future.

These talismans give us hope. They were here before us, and they will be here long after we're gone. And time will only enrich their unfiltered beauty. Take that and stuff it in your selfie.

AUTOMATONS

While shopping at the Brimfield Antique Flea Market in Massachusetts, Blackman stumbled upon a life-size monkey with an apple in his hand. He appeared to be climbing a tree branch, and when picked up, his head nodded. Blackman bought him. He wasn't the only one enamored with the monkey's lifelike demeanor, craftsmanship, and soulful glass eyes. As he walked through the market, treasure in hand, a swarm of dealers followed Blackman to ogle or ask if he'd sell. That peculiar pied piper moment began his fascination with nodders and automatons.

These mechanical wonders are not toys. Meant to be admired, not touched, they're considered an important part of nineteenth-century French art history that incorporates sculpture, painting, costume, and mechanics. For millennia, people like the ancient Egyptians have designed objects capable of movement, but French automatons were a product of the Industrial Revolution. The narrow alleys of the Marais neighborhood in Paris were once home to an array of workshops that manufactured what one observer, in 1867, characterized as "charming frivolities" and "objects of our most capricious fancies."

Blackman came to love and admire those animal automatons specifically made by Roullet & Decamps, who exported their creations all over the world: from Parisian drawing rooms entertaining the glitterati to pashas and maharajas. Over the years, Blackman has built quite a collection—a menagerie that includes smoking monkeys, squealing pigs, lumbering polar bears, musical cats, prowling tigers, and marching elephants.

Most arrive into his care battered and broken. These complex machines with complicated clockwork movements, bellows, and handmade gears are an endangered, rare species that require the skilled hand of an aerospace engineer to bring them back to delight.

BUGATTI

David Cruz heard about a grouping of Carlo Bugatti furniture that surfaced in Mexico. He and Blackman had long admired the Bugatti family. Ettore Bugatti designed cars, and his brother Rembrandt was an artist renowned for his bronze animal sculptures, but it was their father, Carlo, the Milanese designer and creator of experimental art nouveau furnishings, who piqued their interest.

Bugatti's use of organic materials like parchment, vellum, bone, and pounded copper embellished with decorative details—such as tassels and hand-painted images—gave his furnishings a timeless, almost futuristic quality that echoes a mix of Moorish, Moroccan, and Cyrillic motifs.

After securing a hold on the pieces, Cruz and Blackman flew to Mexico City where they met with decorative arts dealer Emmanuel Picault, who had acquired an important collection of Bugatti's work. All the pieces came from one single estate where, many years before, the proprietor—like many members of the Mexican upper classes—traveled to Europe in search of unique pieces to grace their estates.

What they saw was extraordinary. A tall plant stand commissioned around 1906 by the Marchesa Luisa Casati captured their imagination. Casati, an Italian heiress known to parade around with leashed cheetahs and wear snakes as jewelry, was a patron and muse to many artists of her time, including her friend Bugatti. This amazing stand had the name "Casati" in metal prominently inlaid into the base, and Cruz and Blackman couldn't help but envision her coming home, enveloped in snakes, as she glided upstairs to retire for the evening.

Blackman and Cruz planned an opening party for the Bugatti collection, and to their surprise, it was well attended, even though it was September 12, 2001, just one day after the World Trade Center tragedy—a testament that beauty and art can be a salve during tumultuous times.

136

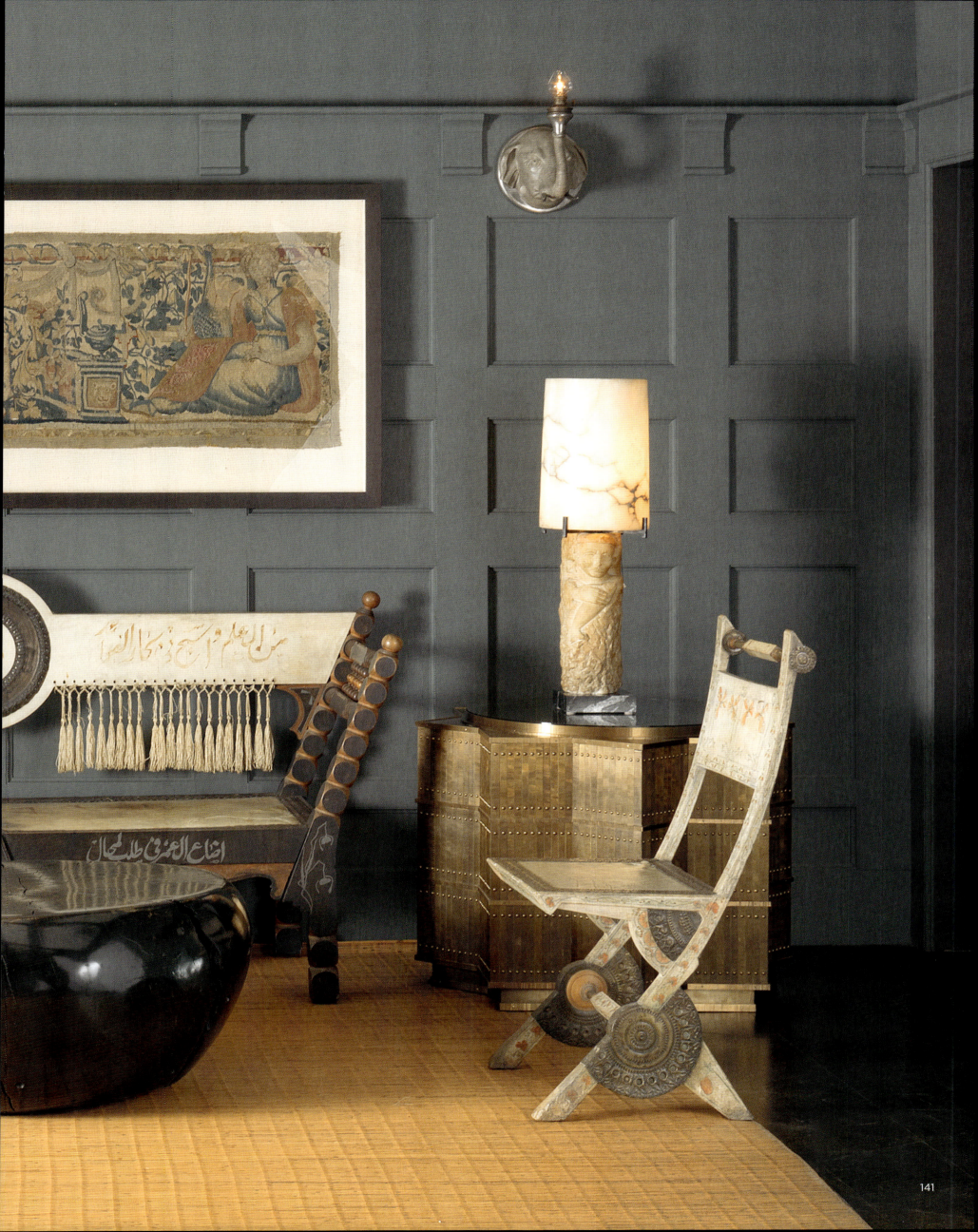

MENDOZA

The Mexico City–based interior designer José "Pepe" Mendoza is known for his brass furniture, lighting, tabletop accessories, and hardware pieces. With their turquoise and malachite-colored ceramic inlay, Mendoza's chunky, modernist interpretations of Mesoamerican glyphs and their healthy proportions evoke Blackman Cruz's fondness for Latin American modernism.

Mendoza's family had a storied history as the manufacturer of arms for General Pancho Villa, who helped lead the Mexican Revolution, which overthrew dictator Porfirio Díaz, and Mendoza used this foundry to produce his work. In 1957, Evelyn and Jerome Ackerman, contemporaries of Charles and Ray Eames, met Mendoza in Mexico City and began distributing his work through their Los Angeles–based ERA Industries.

Like many modernist creatives, the Ackermans were part of the design conversation between Mexico and California that had been going on for decades. In the early 1920s, the Mayan touches on the reliefs of Frank Lloyd Wright's Ennis and Hollyhock Houses signaled that Los Angeles was hospitable to such motifs. Meanwhile, in Mexico City, emigres like Clara Porset from Cuba and Bauhaus veteran Michael van Beuren incorporated Mexican craft into their work, earning national recognition in the 1941 Museum of Modern Art's exhibition *Organic Design in Home Furnishings*. Later, in 1951, esteemed Los Angeles writer Esther McCoy edited an issue heralding Mexican design for the avant-garde *Arts & Architecture* magazine that highlighted architects like Juan O'Gorman and Luis Barragán.

Adam Blackman first saw Mendoza's work in the 1990s—a pedestal table—which he couldn't resist. In a rare coincidence, the table's mate crossed his path a week later, three thousand miles away at his friend Ken Erwin's store, AK1114. That lightning only struck once, and today, Mendoza's work remains as rare as it is recognizable. With its intricate inlay in Aztec and natural forms like fish, birds, seashells, and sunbursts, Mendoza's creations, whether they are brass boxes, tables, lamps, or hardware, continue to keep Blackman Cruz's passion for Pepe alive.

ARTIFACTS & ICONS

In a town that worships at the altar that erases the wrinkles of time, Blackman and Cruz take solace in the old, the weathered, the aged. Such artifacts and iconography earn deference. Evoking the passage of time and lost civilizations, they allow us to witness first-hand histories of sacrifice, rebirth, and the human condition. These universal, secular, and religious themes unite us across temporal boundaries, because we too can experience the same awe and beauty our ancestors did hundreds of years before us.

A nineteenth-century Italian alms box inscribed with the words *memento mori*, or "remember death," may be a bit of emotional blackmail, but it's also a reminder of life cycles, grounding us in the notion that our time is finite, and perhaps we should make the best of it while we're here.

Whether you believe in angels, an afterlife, or that Jesus died for our sins doesn't preclude empathy for the pathos seen on the face of a painstakingly carved wood, eighteenth-century Jesus head, a single tear rolling down his cheek. We all suffer—some are better at it than others—but when we regale the majesty of a Roman marble torso from the second century CE or ponder the lives of the Aztecs as we marvel an architectural relic of that venerable civilization, our imagination sparks, reminding us to respect the elders. We like their lined faces, and they have better stories to tell.

165

ARTURO PANI

It's an exquisite coincidence that Arturo Pani's friends and family called him "el raro," or the rare. His mother gave her queer son the nickname because rather than use a pejorative, she preferred a kinder adjective—an apt metaphor for his extraordinary style. The Mexico City–based interior designer began his career in the 1930s during an era when modernism became the dominant design vernacular, influenced by expats fleeing fascist Europe. Pani differentiated himself with a French-infused glamour that was muscular and flamboyant with sturdy curves, but never spare.

David Cruz discovered Pani in Los Angeles when he and Blackman first opened their shop. Pani, like other Mexican designers who catered to the affluent, was part of a cross-pollination that took place between California and Mexico, especially during the middle of the twentieth century. The pieces he discovered were eccentric and bold—a centipede table or a pair of lamps with bronze-spiked orbs.

Years later, Cruz learned that Pani designed the swank interiors of the art deco landmark Hotel del Prado in Mexico City, where Cruz often met friends for drinks in a salon with a Diego Rivera mural entitled *Dream of a Sunday Afternoon in Alameda Park*. In typical Rivera style, the mural was a cutting commentary on bourgeois society. He also included a self-portrait as a child standing with his wife, Frida Kahlo, towering over him. The hotel didn't survive the 1985 Mexico City earthquake, but the mural did and is now a centerpiece of the Museo Mural Diego Rivera.

Pani's father, a diplomat who took his family to Belgium, Milan, and France, was a Rivera patron and encouraged the painter to leave Paris and travel to Italy, where he studied Renaissance frescoes. Like Rivera, Pani and his older brother Mario studied in Paris. The brothers went to the École des Beaux-Arts, and when he returned to Mexico City in 1935, Arturo and Mario, an architect responsible for some of Mexico City's most iconic buildings, embarked on the first of many collaborations. They designed the Hotel Reforma, where Arturo created an industrial luxuriousness in the public spaces, which became emblematic of Mexican modernism.

Pani continued to work in hospitality, designing interiors and furniture for restaurants and luxury hotels, like the Hotel Bamer, with its circular bar and ample armchairs. Throughout his long career, he used rich materials like parchment, velvet, solid gilded brass, onyx, and mirrors. He often took traditional European styles and gave them his Mexican flair, interpretations that enabled him to gracefully adapt to trends: 1940s Regency, 1950s modernism, and the Swinging 1960s and 1970s, when his Acapulco home epitomized what became known as "Acapulco style," and was captured in an iconic image by society photographer Slim Aarons.

PAGE 121
CLOCKWISE FROM TOP LEFT: *Pair of Blackman Cruz Workshop (BCW) Eclipse Sconces; BCW Constellation Mirror; Roullet & Decamps smoking monkey for Louis Vuitton, ca. 1906; BCW Tower Side Table; French leather lounge chair, ca. 1940; Parabellum medicine ball for Blackman Cruz*

AUTOMATONS

PAGE 123
Collection of automatons and nodders, 1870–1940

PAGES 124–125
LEFT TO RIGHT: *Roullet & Decamps elephant automaton; Mexican carved polychromed wood-carnival elephant; Roullet & Decamps elephant automaton; Roullet & Decamps elephant automaton*

PAGES 126–127
LEFT TO RIGHT: *Roullet & Decamps drumming bear automatons; nineteenth-century monkey nodder; Napoleonic smoking monkey and monkey chef automatons*

BUGATTI

PAGE 129
Detail of Carlo Bugatti throne chair

PAGE 130
TOP: *Carlo Bugatti signature* • BOTTOM: *Rare Rembrandt Bugatti drawing in Carlo Bugatti frame, Italy, ca. 1900*

PAGE 131
TOP TO BOTTOM: *Monumental Carlo Bugatti vitrine; pair of Fontana Arte sconces; bronze figure; Alison Berger glass water vessels, exclusively for Blackman Cruz; three Miguel Berrocal puzzle sculptures; nineteenth-century marble foot fragment; contemporary angular vase by Dougall Paulson; nineteenth-century French sculpting stands; Clarke & Reilly daybed*

PAGE 132
LEFT TO RIGHT: *Carlo Bugatti armchair; live model in Carlo Bugatti side chair*

PAGE 133
Carlo Bugatti side chair in found condition

PAGE 134
Carlo Bugatti throne chair

PAGE 135
Carlo Bugatti lamp table

PAGE 136
LEFT: *Carlo Bugatti side chair* • RIGHT: *Carlo Bugatti stand from the estate of Marchesa Luisa Casati*

PAGE 137
Collection of Carlo Bugatti chair finials

PAGES 138–139
Carlo Bugatti settee in found condition

PAGES 140–141
CLOCKWISE FROM TOP LEFT: *Pair of BCW Ganesh Sconces; framed tapestry fragment; pair of Spanish carved alabaster table lamps; pair of Damian Jones Seren side tables; Carlo Bugatti side chair; Japanese bamboo tatami mat; Carlo Bugatti settee from the estate of Marchesa Luisa Casati; Dan Pollock coffee table; Carlo Bugatti throne chair*

MENDOZA

PAGE 143
TOP TO BOTTOM: *Pepe Mendoza eye lamp; antique French chopping block*

PAGES 144–145
Collection of Pepe Mendoza dishes

PAGE 146
TOP: *Pair of Pepe Mendoza Orientalist table lamps* • BOTTOM: *Glass-top Pepe Mendoza side table*

PAGE 147
Pepe Mendoza coffee table

PAGE 148
TOP TO BOTTOM: *Collection of large Pepe Mendoza bowls and platters; Austrian brass bowl; Pepe Mendoza drawer pull*

PAGE 149
TOP TO BOTTOM: *de Sede lounge chair; Mike Moses (1898–1973) bronze sculpture; Pepe Mendoza side table*

ARTIFACTS & ICONS

PAGE 151
Nineteenth-century Italian painted wood memento mori collection tray

PAGES 152–153
Nineteenth-century Mexican silver crown of thorns

PAGE 154
Gilded silver and gold repoussé auras

PAGE 155
Eighteenth-century northern European wood Jesus

PAGE 156
Italian seventeenth-century alabaster Saint Sebastian

PAGE 157
Italian eighteenth-century ivory crucifix

PAGE 158
Detail of Oaxacan eighteenth-century polychromed-wood crucifix

PAGE 159
Oaxacan eighteenth-century polychromed-wood crucifix from the collection of Enrique Romero

PAGE 160
Model with pair of Mike Diaz Patria wood altar sticks

PAGE 161
Early twentieth-century monumental Chinese processional pagoda

PAGE 162
TOP TO BOTTOM: *Antique framed mirror; Roman bronze arm fragment; BCW Deliquescent Dining Table*

PAGE 163
Second-century CE Roman marble torso

PAGE 164
TOP TO BOTTOM: *Teotihuacan pre-Columbian vessel, round wood tray; pre-Columbian carved shell*

PAGE 165
Basalt Aztec carving

ARTURO PANI

PAGE 167
CLOCKWISE FROM TOP LEFT: *BCW Primal Mirror; BCW Ganesh Sconce; José Luis Cuevas (1934–2017) Cuatro Prostitutas de Acapulco drawings; BCW Figural Lamp; BCW Bombe Chest; Arturo Pani dining set; glass wine vessels*

PAGE 168
Arturo Pani pendant fixture

PAGE 169
Pair of Arturo Pani occasional tables, Mexico, ca. 1955

PAGE 170
TOP TO BOTTOM: *Detail; Arturo Pani dining table*

PAGE 171
Pair of Arturo Pani floor lamps from the Reforma Hotel

PAGE 172
Arturo Pani dining table

Chapter 3

HABITATS

"Fun and sexy are not applicable to décor. Sex should be sexy. Fun can be sex. But interiors should be comfortable and reveal themselves slowly and sensually." —Paul Fortune

The late Paul Fortune was a friend, a client, and an interior designer with an irreverent flair. His laissez-faire attitude allowed him to indulge his impeccable taste for an array of residential and hospitality clients. He lived as he worked, settling into the daily pace of life with a democratic approach to comfort; he fed the neighborhood squirrels, and if the cat clawed the upholstery, he let it be. And like Blackman Cruz, Fortune's standards eschewed trends and notions of perfection in favor of authentic interiors that withstand the passage of time.

As antique dealers, Adam Blackman and David Cruz are in the business of filling domestic spaces with memorable pieces that spark recognition in their clients. Yes, that dazzling Italian iron-and-brass cocktail table is a must-have, and without those nineteenth-century fluted columns, the living room will be a bore. Such attraction to furniture and objets d'art that offer both form and function may be as individual as a fingerprint, but isn't that how we should live, by the whims of our own tastes?

In their homes, Blackman and Cruz subscribe to the same philosophy. Much like the inventory in the shop, Cruz's Los Angeles house is an evolving, multicentury laboratory. A 1970s Italian leather couch might make a cameo in the living room, and then it's gone. But he has a few attachments, like Jeff Price's earthy sculpture, which some might interpret as a phallus; the Roman sundial, which he acquired after coveting it for a decade; and, of course, the Paul László house, with an open, generous floor plan that accommodates Cruz's multiple iterations. In Mexico, his colonial nineteenth-century house, with thick stone and adobe walls, has been updated with a contemporary addition, creating an inescapable structural relationship between history and style, and the past and present.

For Blackman, his interiors reflect and provide a counterpoint to mid-century architecture and his appetite for collecting. In his Los Angeles A. Quincy Jones–designed home, automatons and Pepe Mendoza lamps are touchstones, yet there are surprises, like a Venetian glass mirror in the entry and a pond filled with plump goldfish. In Ojai, the ever-changing, seasonal palette of the mountain range and sensory cues like the intoxicating scent of spring orange blossoms drive the design toward a sense of place. A blue 1960s Jetboard may adorn a wall, but the real luxury is a seat in the garden where pollinating bees buzz and colorful butterflies flutter, poignant reminders of ephemeral cycles.

In many ways, furnishing a house is like planting a garden. A series of choices, like seeds burrowed in the ground, eventually bloom into an expression of who we are, what we like, and how we want to live. Such monoculture-defying variety is the Blackman Cruz spirit; otherwise, shouldn't we all just check-in to a generic hotel and call it a life?

ADAM BLACKMAN

Los Angeles

When Adam Blackman and his wife, Kate, a graphic designer, bought their 1950 post-and-beam home in the Crestwood Hills neighborhood of Los Angeles, they weren't looking for a pedigreed mid-century modern house. Blackman had hopes for an industrial space he could customize, and his wife preferred something more traditional in style. But when they saw the house by architect A. Quincy Jones, they were enamored with the design and the neighborhood's rich history.

Established in 1946 by four friends—musicians recently discharged from the army—the Mutual Housing Association realized a vision for a cooperative residential community that would bring good design to middle-class families. Hundreds pooled their resources to purchase the hillside acreage and hire architects A. Quincy Jones and Whitney R. Smith to plan the neighborhood. The modernist outpost would eventually be known as Crestwood Hills and grow to include homes by Richard Neutra, Craig Ellwood, Rodney Walker, and Ray Kappe, among others.

Over the decades, the architectural bonds of the community would be tested by the fury of Mother Nature (the infamous 1961 Bel Air Fire) and the push and pull of changing lifestyles. Although the couple's house suffered an unfortunate 1980s redo, its bones remained solid and relatively untouched. The Blackmans set out to preserve it and bring it back to its modernist core. They sought a partner who would embrace the simple beauty of the home's original materials and hired the Los Angeles–based firm RAC Design Build to help them recapture the architect's original intent.

Over the next two years, RAC would gently peel back the misplaced layers of stucco, brass fittings, and thick, white paint to uncover the home's sweet notes—a long-forgotten louvered wall between the living room and library, the violet hue of the original cinder block, and the interplay of pattern and color found in the generous use of redwood and Douglas fir. The 1980s additions were reconfigured and simplified to revive the indoor-outdoor flow so indicative of the community's mandate to harmonize with its natural surroundings.

The home's celebration of clean lines and honest materials provides an elegant backdrop to some of Blackman's most favored pieces—the wavy silhouette of the bronze and caned Gazelle dining set by Dan Johnson keeps good company with the organic flair of a painted work by Claire Falkenstein and found objects like a fallen and unfinished Sevres urn, now cherished for the very same imperfections. While the cabinets display an ever-evolving outpouring of objects by makers known and unknown, the living areas of the home are furnished to support the defining character of the construction materials. Case in point: a quiet collection of Chinese water carriers adorns a new cinderblock wall in the kitchen, while the bed in the primary bedroom, a custom walnut and brass design by Rick Cortez, underscores the visual rhythm of the natural pattern on the Douglas fir closet doors.

When Julius Schulman, the famed modernist photographer, returned to Crestwood Hills decades later to shoot the Blackman home, he pronounced that Jones would have approved of the resulting living space for its success at blurring the old with the new. The house would go on to be awarded Historic Cultural Monument status by the city of Los Angeles and recognized as architecturally significant by the Hammer Museum through its inclusion in the retrospective *A. Quincy Jones: Building for Better Living*.

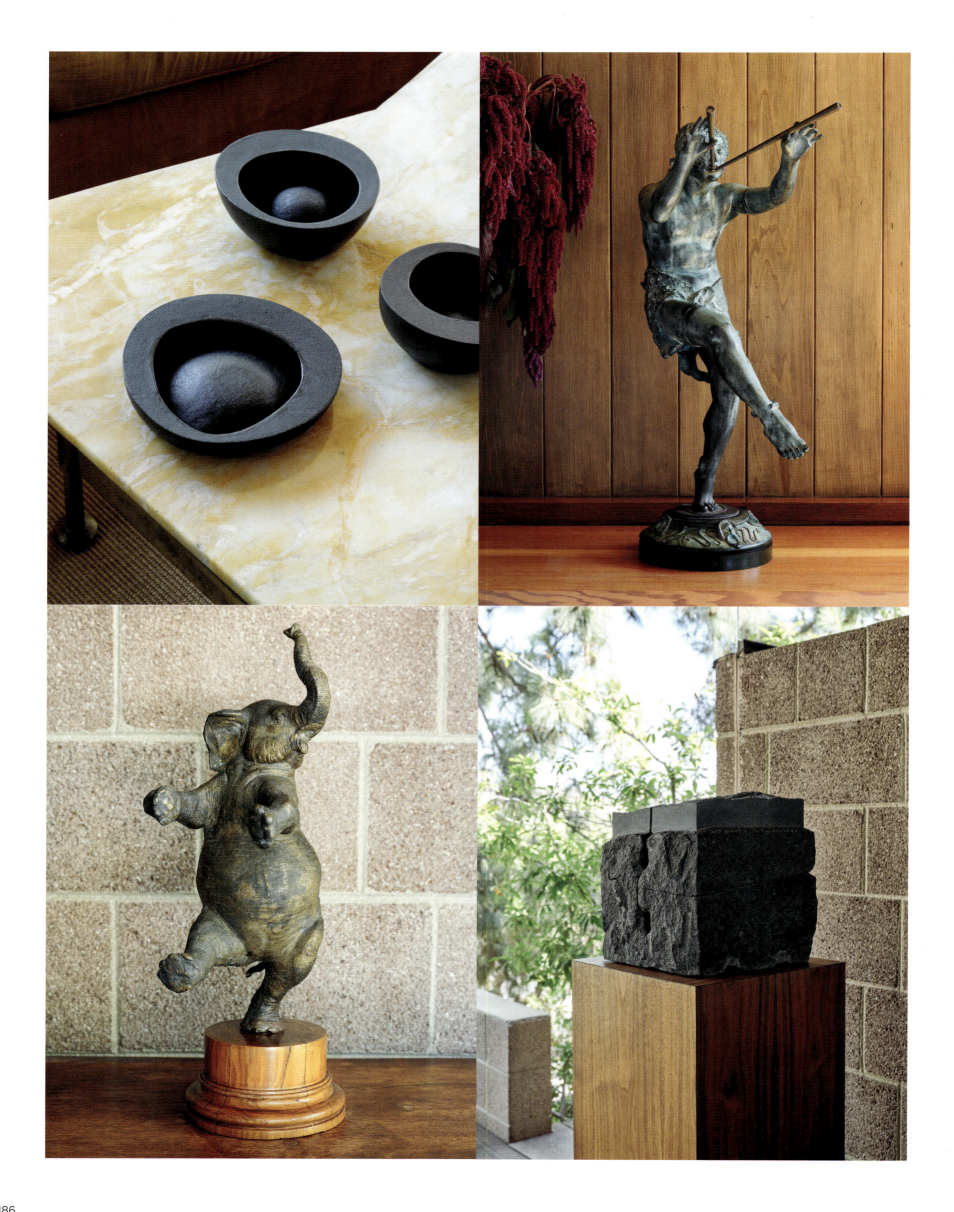

ADAM BLACKMAN

Ojai

When seeking a respite from city life, Blackman and his wife retreat to their home in Ojai, California, where luminous pink sunsets, idyllic stone walls, and fragrant citrus groves abound. With its rare east-west orientation, some believe the Ojai Valley is an energetic vortex. In the early 1900s, spiritualists like the Theosophists settled there. Later, philosopher Jiddu Krishnamurti attracted artists, writers, and musicians like Jackson Pollock, Aldous Huxley, John Lennon, Yoko Ono, and Jimi Hendrix. Ojai continues to draw freethinkers and New Age enthusiasts, but it is also notable for its architecture—century-old Spanish-style landmarks, the result of a wintering industrialist's imaginings of what a rural enclave should look like, and homes by Julia Morgan (of Hearst Castle fame), Paul Revere Williams, and Greene and Greene, among others.

The Blackmans, looking for a new project, were unaware of the valley's intriguing origins when they stumbled upon what would become their home away from home—a quirky compound surrounded by an unexpected, mature garden. But something about the views of the Topatopa Mountain Range, with its famous Chief Peak, the Jurassic-size agaves, and majestic California oaks, took hold instantly.

The original owner, a modernist enthusiast, designed and built the main house in 1959—seemingly by his own hand. Aerial photographs from the period revealed the mid-century home was the first to be built in an area dominated by sagebrush and orange groves. Over the years, the home would be reconfigured and expanded many times, adding to its rustic charm.

Ample windows capture Ojai's magical, warm light and look out onto an acre of sprawling gardens with cactus, fruit trees, and lots of California native plantings. Hidden behind stone walls, the landscape is dotted with outdoor sculpture and vintage pieces—a bronze cherub fountain by the preeminent nineteenth-century sculptress Janet Scudder, a pair of seventeenth-century Italian stone mooring posts (now used as stools), a 1980s cast bronze sculpture entitled *Tornado* by Mark Lere, a nineteenth-century stone cistern, and a massive terra-cotta planter from 1965 by David Cressey for Architectural Pottery. Stone paths, some created by the Blackmans and some by the previous owner, intersect and wind throughout.

Indoors, the choices are purposefully low-key, as this is a place where family and friends gather. Pepe Mendoza makes an appearance, as does a Blackman Cruz Workshop (BCW) 3-Squared Chandelier over the dining room table. A handwrought iron fire screen that reminded Blackman of a country cabin is offset by a prototype of the bronze BCW Drip Coffee Table surrounded by a suite of de Sede lounge chairs. In the studio, a sofa and monumental, two-tiered marble coffee table by designer Kerry Joyce are new additions, and no Blackman residence would be complete without an animal presence. Behold Wally, the papier-mâché walrus.

ADAM BLACKMAN • LA

PAGE 179
The five stones in the courtyard represent the five elements in Buddhist thought—earth, water, fire, wind, and void

PAGE 180
TOP: *Art wall separating the original home and new addition* • BOTTOM: *Bed cover (gifted for the couple's wedding chuppah from friend Pat McGann); nineteenth-century Japanese watercolor*

PAGE 181
TOP: *Montici coffee table; Mies van der Rohe daybed; Bill Hinz tapestry, Chicago Playboy Club; Manchester-by-the-Sea watercolor by Anna Hayward, Kate's great-grandmother* • BOTTOM: *Marble wings, top of the "never sell" list*

PAGES 182–183
Custom-designed windows by Rick Cortez; Papa Bear chair by Hans Wegner; Blackman Cruz Workshop (BCW) Record Table

PAGE 184
The kitchen, once an outdoor patio, connects the office to the sitting room

PAGE 185
Venetian mirror, discovered in Paris; desk from the Mercanteinfiera Antiques Fair in Parma, Italy

PAGE 186
CLOCKWISE FROM TOP LEFT: *Ashtrays designed by Isamu Noguchi; Gio Ponti coffee table;* The Flute Player *by Eugène Désiré Piron, ca. 1905; granite sculpture by Seiji Kunishima (b. 1937) entitled* Stone Work 79-1*; Andrea Spadini (1912–1983) bronze elephant maquette for the Delacorte Clock at the Tisch Children's Zoo in Central Park, New York*

PAGE 187
Cabinet of curiosities

PAGE 188
TOP: *Adam's 1972 Maserati Merak* • BOTTOM: *Bronze nude with lute by Ted Randall (1914–1985)*

PAGE 189
Pond, filled with feeder goldfish

ADAM BLACKMAN • OJAI

PAGE 191
Cupid and Tortoise, *bronze fountain by Janet Scudder (1869–1940)*

PAGES 192–193
Oak and pepper trees abound

PAGE 194
Wool tapestry by Pablo Picasso (1881–1973); BCW 3-Squared Chandelier

PAGE 195
TOP: *Antique casement windows; eighteenth-century wood floor; Sarouk rug from Adam's grandparents' Bronx home; Kerry Joyce-designed sofa and coffee table; aluminum-clad Jetboard, 1965* • BOTTOM: *Jean-Boris Lacroix floor lamp, two paintings by Eric Orr (1939–1998)*

PAGE 196
Wally, the French, papier-mâché walrus with glass eyes; five-drawer plywood chest; eighteenth-century Régence urn

PAGE 197
Wood and ceramic bones

PAGE 198
Rusty brutalist sculptures, artist unknown

PAGE 199
Twelve-foot weathered-plank table

DAVID CRUZ

Los Angeles

David Cruz and his husband, writer and director Richard Hochberg, live in Whitley Heights, a neighborhood that harkens back to the golden age of Hollywood. Developed close to the studios in 1910s and 1920s, it quickly became a haven for celebrities like Rudolf Valentino, Louise Brooks, and Gloria Swanson, and writers like William Faulkner and F. Scott Fitzgerald, who came to LA to work in movies. Later, Bette Davis moved in, joining others like Anita Loos, the first female screenwriter, who authored *Gentleman Prefer Blondes*.

Beyond the historic Hollywood charm and a Mediterranean flair, today the neighborhood is listed in the National Register of Historic Places, a welcome time capsule with intact period architecture untainted by Los Angeles's rampant mansionization. Cruz's international-style home stands out among the Italianate and Spanish-revival stylings of its neighbors. Built in 1939 by Hungarian-born Paul László, the home, with its flat roof, glass brick, and a "moat of air" that separates the house from the street, was commissioned by László's friend Dr. Hans Schiff. Like László, Schiff was Jewish, had celebrity clients, and fled Nazi Germany for Los Angeles.

László later opened a showroom on Rodeo Drive in Beverly Hills and built a successful architecture, furniture, and interiors practice, honing his luxurious modernist style for affluent clientele. Cruz's house, designed just a year after László arrived in Los Angeles, is anomalous to his later work. But its unadorned modernist quality, with an approachable whiff of luxury, like the cantilevered deck with twinkling city views, serves Cruz well. Like László, Cruz subscribes to a beauty-over-ideology design philosophy, and he changes the furnishings often, sating his need for reinvention. Currently, the house contains a pair of generously proportioned László chairs and some Arturo Pani lamps, but except for a couple antiquities—a Roman torso and sundial and some pre-Columbian pieces—the house is an ever-changing tableau that pleases the whims of his visual palette.

DAVID CRUZ

San Miguel de Allende, Mexico

In the Mexican city of San Miguel de Allende, David Cruz and Richard Hochberg recently renovated a traditional nineteenth-century house along a picturesque cobblestone street. The house, which offers the couple an opportunity to spend more time in Cruz's native Mexico, has a view of the iconic neo-Gothic pink sandstone church that marks the zocalo, or city center, which UNESCO deems a World Heritage Site.

When the Spanish arrived in the sixteenth century, the region was a stronghold during Mexico's war of independence with Spain, and the city was later named after revolutionary war hero Ignacio Allende. Since the 1930s, San Miguel de Allende has attracted bohemian expats, and recent archaeological discoveries denote the existence of a complex pre-Columbian society.

Cruz contrasted the home's colonial roots with traditional twentieth-century Mexican themes, opting for a multicentury aesthetic conversation. The project also allowed him to work with Mexican colleagues and friends. Interior designer Claudia Grajales of CORE studio designed the contemporary kitchen and encouraged Cruz to use salvaged, volcanic stone to create a generous staircase leading to the pool. Architect Juan Elías Robledo collaborated with Cruz to open up the living room and design dramatic, modern staircases that capture light, casting pleasing shadows that change as the sun moves through the sky.

When he furnished the house, Cruz used a similar past-meets-present philosophy, incorporating pieces from contemporary Mexican designers, like horsehair stools by Guadalajara-based artist Aldo Alvarez Tostado, as well as mid-century Butaque chairs by William Spratling. The living room is anchored by a pair of chunky couches by architect Francisco Artigas, a favorite of Cruz, known for the impeccable modernist homes he designed in the El Pedregal neighborhood of Mexico City. A nineteenth-century Mexican interpretation of Biedermeier, replete with a carved snake border, a wood inlaid eighteenth-century cabinet from Puebla, Mexico, and some significant pre-Columbian artifacts add tradition to the mix.

For many years, Cruz channeled his tastes through a Eurocentric lens. His rekindled friendship with Mexico has inspired an aesthetic exploration in a country with a complicated colonial history.

DAVID CRUZ • LA

PAGE 201
Nite River *by Patricia Larsen*

PAGES 202–203
TOP LEFT & TOP RIGHT: *Julius Shulman photographs; architecture by Paul László; house built in 1939* • BOTTOM LEFT: *Dining room: 1930s Murano chandelier; pair of Leucos lamps; pre-Columbian stone figure; Carlo de Carli chairs; Blackman Cruz Workshop (BCW) Op table* • BOTTOM RIGHT: *Kitchen: Hallworth Design, Roman sundial*

PAGE 204
Piano room: 1914 rare Josef Hoffmann armchair; Scandinavian piano; French art deco light fixture; theatrical stage drawing

PAGE 205
Living Room: Harush Shlomo studded aluminum seat, Israel, 2005; French 1930s buffet; 1970s French wingback armchairs; oversized Buddha hands; Ashanti stool: This room is a case where less would have been more.

PAGE 206
Eighteenth-century Puebla marquetry cabinet; marble grand tour foot; graphite sketches of feet

PAGE 207
TOP LEFT: *Leucos 1970s table lamp; nineteenth-century oil of male nude; nineteenth-century graphite life drawing sketches* • TOP RIGHT: *David Alfaro Siqueiros charcoal sketch for Mexico City mural; ancient Greek kylix; lamps by Dominique Heidenberg; Jean Touret buffet, 1958* • BOTTOM LEFT: *Charlie (the much-missed pet)* • BOTTOM RIGHT: *Shoji screens and Thebes barstool*

PAGE 208
1930s French night stand; photograph of David's mother, Catalina Russek Gameros

PAGE 209
László banister; nineteenth-century staircase maquette

PAGE 210
TOP LEFT: *Jeff Price sculpture* • TOP RIGHT: *Paul László banister; mysterious and anonymous marble urn* • BOTTOM: *Set of pre-Columbian inspired glyphs from Emmanuel Picault's glamorous gallery, Chic by Accident*

PAGE 211
Headless Roman bust

DAVID CRUZ •
SAN MIGUEL DE ALLENDE, MEXICO

PAGE 212
Portrait of David Cruz and Richard Hochberg

PAGE 213
Cantera-stone entrance

PAGES 214 & 215
Architecture by Juan Elías Robledo

PAGE 216
Kitchen by Claudia Grajales, founder of Core, San Miguel de Allende; hanging light by Thierry Jeannot

PAGE 217
From the bedroom to the kitchen

PAGES 218–219
Living room entrance

PAGE 220
Early twentieth-century Oaxacan mezcal vessels

PAGE 221
Tracking the Stars by Patricia Larsen; Francisco Artigas couch; BCW Peyote Chairs; Beni rug

PAGE 222
Backyard and pool and environs

PAGE 223
The couple's first San Miguel house, with a Jacuzzi and panoramic view of the town

Chapter 4

BLACKMAN CRUZ WORKSHOP

"A chair is a very difficult object. A skyscraper is almost easier. That is why Chippendale is famous."
—Ludwig Mies van der Rohe

Blackman, Cruz, and creative director Lika Moore have designed and manufactured their own pieces since 1998. The Blackman Cruz Workshop (BCW), an ever-evolving collection of objects, furniture, and lighting, indulges their stylistic predilections, offering a contemporary complement to the decorative arts in the showroom.

These crafted pieces play with the past without becoming pastiche. The plaster Primal Lighting line pays homage to French designers and artists from the 1920s and 1930s, who looked to abstract forms of African art and sculpture. The Molar Stool has a kinetic, teethy quality, and zoomorphic forms entice as the bronze-cast Rattler table slithers into the mix. The Under Pressure Sconce has David Bowie and the ever-feeding multibreasted Roman goddess Diana on the mind. Meanwhile, rococo extravagance is reinterpreted in the hefty bronze-and-glass Deliquescent Table.

BCW designs also take cues from biomorphic forms, delving into functional surrealism. The earthy Peyote Chair in shearling is soft like its spineless namesake cactus, while the limited-edition marble Leary Drip Table (as in Timothy), with its drop formations that mimic water, implies things may not be as they seem, because they never are.

Some pieces are designed to entertain. The Tickler Table Lamp has a playful name and looks a little naughty. The elephantine face of the Ganesh Wall Sconce appears to burst through the wall, and the animated Thieving Monkey Sconce looks as if he might hop into your lap and swipe your popcorn. And why not bring the circus home? These days we could all use a little entertainment.

251

252

LIKA MOORE

Lika Moore has been part of the Blackman Cruz team since 1998. Back then, she, Cruz, and Blackman worked in the small West Hollywood showroom with one computer and a fax machine. Today, she helps guide the business's visual identity and plays an integral design role in the Blackman Cruz Workshop (BCW).

Moore channels her fascination with ancient cultures into creations that possess a bold splendor. She designs jewelry, lighting, and furniture inspired by the intricate craftsmanship of Baroque navigation implements; Polynesian oceanic adornments; tools made from bone, feathers and wood; and classical forms like the grounding femininity of a cabriole leg.

Her process can be fearless. In 2015, when Blackman Cruz and Chicago-based Wright auction house staged an exhibition and sale, Moore took a 12-gauge shotgun to her Leonine Wall Console, conjuring the force of Mother Nature's ability to corrode, weather, and pit. She preserved this harsh patina in bronze with hand patination. The result of her labor: a one-of-a-kind design that pays homage to Greek mythology and the fierce stance of a lioness, which in Moore's eyes, becomes a predator of beauty.

She explored her attraction to earth elements, like fire, in a 2021 collaboration with the British design atelier Clarke & Reilly. For a wall piece entitled *The Beginning*, she linked myth to antiquity by resurrecting the process of Roman mirror making. She used fire to polish and blast steel, fashioning an ellipse-shaped visual portal that prods the eye to consider other dimensions.

Such play with time and orientation also spawned her Compass Series, which references contemplative, personal, and aesthetic journeys. The series began with a simple, four-pronged, squat bronze candlestick. Like any trip, it took some turns and grew into the grounded Herkimer Table Lamp, morphed into the sculptural Compass Sconce, and landed as a key embellishment on the Compass Dressing Mirror, reflecting back the stops along the way.

Her commitment to a constantly evolving design practice makes for work that never stands still. For her Brass Ball Series, the physical act of illumination inspired the mechanization. Crafted from tropical wood, polished brass, and silk, each variation requires a different method to coax it along—a gentle touch or a firm twist of the brass ball—turns it on. An early design, the now-classic BCW Triball Lamp, has had many iterations, and during a Sotheby's London auction for antique dealer Gordon Watson, the frenzied response marked her work as iconic.

PAGE 227
Blackman Cruz Workshop (BCW) Moon Sconce

PAGES 228–229
LEFT TO RIGHT: *Antique textiles from Pat McGann; BCW Deliquescent Dining Table; BCW Constellation Mirror; BCW Sisyphus Bookends; BCW Large Horizontal Studded Table Lamp by Lika Moore; Alison Berger water vessel exclusively for Blackman Cruz; creamware pitcher; BCW Piranhas in bronze; Japanese ikebana usubata; Jeff Price bronze heart for Blackman Cruz; BCW Horny Lamp; BCW Brutalist Prickets; live snakes*

PAGE 230
CLOCKWISE FROM TOP LEFT: *Framed pre-Columbian Peruvian textile; Pequod Floor Lamp by Jane Hallworth; BCW Peyote Chair; BCW Leary Side Table in marble*

PAGE 231
Detail of BCW Peyote Chair

PAGE 232
BCW Record Table created to honor the vinyl record

PAGE 233
LEFT TO RIGHT: *BCW Under Pressure Sconce; BCW Tree Trunk Table; Roullet & Decamps smoking monkey automaton dressed as Napoleon, ca. 1870*

PAGES 234–235
CLOCKWISE FROM TOP LEFT: *Pair of BCW Salamander Sconces; BCW Crown of Thorns Mirror; pair of BCW Prana Hand Andirons sculpted by Adam Kurtzman; BCW Gothic Console; Phulkari textile*

PAGE 236
TOP, CLOCKWISE FROM TOP LEFT: *Pair of BCW Ganesh Sconces; BCW Compass Mirror by Lika Moore; Moroccan throw rug; Syrian inlaid armchair; BCW Op Table; Spanish 1970s wire-mesh rhinoceros* • BOTTOM, LEFT TO RIGHT: *Pair of nineteenth-century Venetian club chairs; BCW Leonine Garden Table by Lika Moore; contemporary stone and glass vessels;* The Beginning *by Lika Moore*

PAGE 237
TOP LEFT, TOP TO BOTTOM: *BCW Compass Dressing Mirror by Lika Moore* •

TOP RIGHT: *BCW Ganesh Sconce* • BOTTOM LEFT: *BCW Mushroom Table* • BOTTOM RIGHT, TOP TO BOTTOM: *BCW Brutalist Prickets; BCW Talon Table*

PAGE 238
TOP TO BOTTOM: *Brutalist verdigris wall sculpture; BCW Tazza Bowl; BCW Whitley Console Cabinet*

PAGE 239
TOP, LEFT TO RIGHT: *Pair of BCW Compass Sconces; BCW Dakota Lamps, crown of thorns tramp art mirror; stone sculpture in the style of H. R. Giger* • BOTTOM, LEFT TO RIGHT: *Harlech Credenza by Damian Jones; BCW Herkimer Table Lamp; Carlo Bugatti armchair; BCW Olympian Torchiere*

PAGE 240
Detail of BCW Athena Table

PAGE 241
BCW Skull Lamp

PAGES 242–243
LEFT TO RIGHT: *Pair of Max Ingrand for Fontana Arte sconces; nineteenth-century Chinese altar table; pair of BCW Large Studded Table Lamps by Lika Moore; two-panel Japanese wave screen;* Prowling Monkey *by Emma Rodgers; large Campo del Cielo meteorite; nineteenth-century Italian bronze and leather Savonarola chair*

PAGE 244
BCW 3-Squared Chandeliers in different finishes

PAGE 245
BCW Chaak Chest

PAGE 246
LEFT TO RIGHT: *Spanish eighteenth-century writing table; model; BCW Vertebrae Lamp from the Primal Collection*

PAGE 247
LEFT TO RIGHT: *Clarke & Reilly center table; BCW Wedge Table Lamp; BCW Tickler Table Lamp; BCW Primal Lighting Collection: Wedge, Tickler, Ribbed, Webbed*

PAGE 248
Detail of BCW Bombe Chest

PAGE 249
LEFT TO RIGHT: *Carlo Bugatti side chair; BCW Bombe Chest; nineteenth-century Italian framed mirror; carved stone torso*

PAGE 250
BCW Rattler Table

PAGE 251
BCW Snake Chair, sculpted by Malaki Kindred

PAGE 252
TOP: *Pair of BCW Hand Sconces sculpted by Malaki Kindred* • BOTTOM, TOP TO BOTTOM: *BCW Viga Table Lamps; carved stone capitals*

PAGE 253
TOP TO BOTTOM: *BCW 3-Squared Monumental Chandelier; spectacular pair of bronze doors; pair of BCW Olympian Torchieres; BCW Tazza Candleholders; pair of BCW Sillon Chairs; BCW Mushroom Table; pair of Gaetano Pesce stools*

PAGE 254
LEFT TO RIGHT: *BCW Skull Lamp in nickel; BCW Jester's Mirror in aluminum; collection of Alison Berger water vessels*

PAGE 255
BCW Molar Stool

LIKA MOORE

PAGE 256
Blackman Cruz Tenth Anniversary Sphere by Lika Moore

PAGE 257
The Beginning *by Lika Moore*

PAGE 258
Detail of BCW Triball Lamp

PAGE 259
BCW Triball Lamp

PAGE 260
BCW Leonine Wall Console

PAGE 261
Detail of BCW Leonine Wall Console

PAGE 262
LEFT TO RIGHT: *Boulder Table by Preston Sharp; two Japanese ikebana usubata; BCW Compass Candlesticks by Lika Moore; nineteenth-century Japanese bronze articulated lobster*

Chapter 5

COMRADES

"Too much of a good thing can be wonderful." —Mae West

Over the years, Blackman Cruz has represented artists who believe design is not static and community matters. The interaction between the artisans and the showroom is visual and social, a friendship where the exchange bursts forth in an engaging aesthetic conversation that challenges traditional design tropes.

These comrades add a contemporary layer to the antiques on the showroom floor. They may use common materials, like bronze, wood, leather, iron, and found objects, but with innovation comes elevation, drawing inspiration from classic, modern, ancient, and organic forms. Like a great party, these pieces add another curious point of view that makes the mix even more entertaining.

Gianni Vallino, who assembles lighting from cast-off manufacturing debris, disrupts our notions of waste. Thierry Jeannot transforms plastic bottles into glimmering chandeliers, and Mike Diaz imbues his vivid imagination into pieces handmade by Mexican craftspeople. Jane Hallworth's ethereal, narrative lighting has a supernatural elegance. When you put all these voices together, one can't help but admire the daring, inventive mind of the maker.

Whether they be political, aesthetic, or humorous, these creators all have strong opinions. And like members of any family, their idiosyncratic styles enrich the whole with spirited contributions.

GIANNI VALLINO

Italian-born Gianni Vallino transforms cast-off industrial parts into his elegant lighting designs. A self-taught assembler influenced by European philosophers Theodor Adorno and Günter Anders, as well as Dadaism and the avant-garde Situationist International movement, Vallino peels back the curtain on capitalistic manufacturing values, revealing that in his hands, upcycled production waste has aesthetic value.

Working in his central California studio, he reclaims what society discards, redefining conventional ideas about the meaning of value and inserting his work into the conversation about art and craft with a new ecological aesthetic.

Vallino hunts for parts like a post-industrial archaeologist, excavating fragments from medical equipment, rockets that deliver satellites into space, aeronautical remnants, and even bicycle parts. Made of substantive materials like brass, bronze, aluminum, and vulcanized natural rubber, his spontaneous assemblage disrupts the constant flow of consumption, and the pieces shine like gems, unearthed from a world drowning in waste, each a unique expression of the material and the subversive approach of the creator.

MIKE DIAZ

Mike Diaz was born on the US-Mexican border, where the austerity of an expansive gray-and-beige desert landscape drew him to the flamboyant architecture of seventeenth- and eighteenth-century Mexican baroque. It ignited his imagination with visions of intricate facades, gilded ornamentation, and horror vacui, the fear of empty space. Diaz's fascination with Japanese mingei folk art, Sicilian baroque design, as well as Mexican art deco and indigenous iconography, define his more-is-more approach.

Restraint may not be part of Diaz's visual vocabulary, but classical improvisations using artisans in his workshops in Michoacán and Guerrero, Mexico, result in one-of-a-kind, theatrical pieces, which he imagines should have existed historically.

Made from upcycled pine salvaged from structures, some as old as three hundred years, his rustic heirlooms are hand-carved, leaving the natural attributes of the wood grain intact. Sustainably finished with natural beeswax and linseed oil stains, his work has an organic veneer, with a narrative that crosses temporal boundaries.

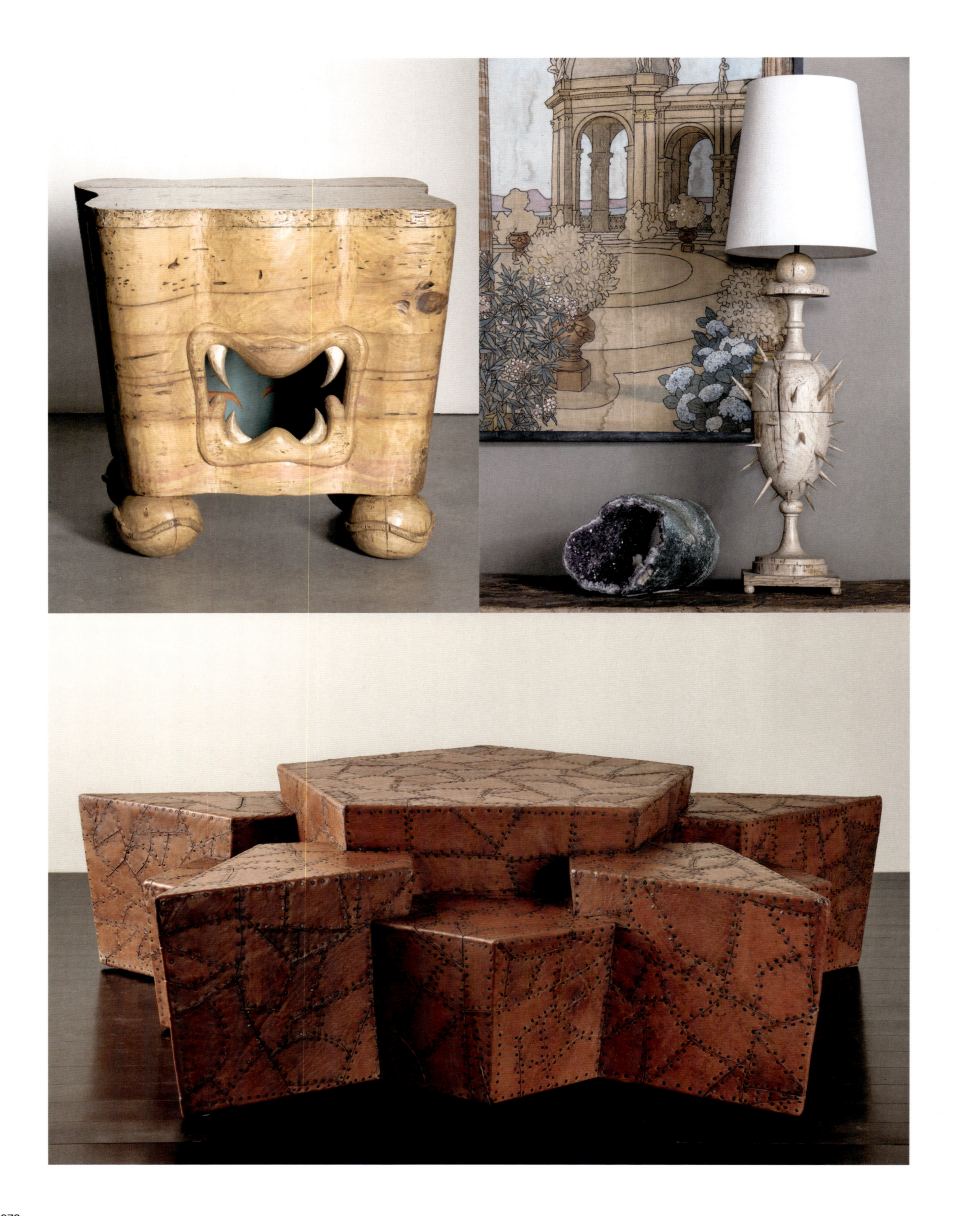

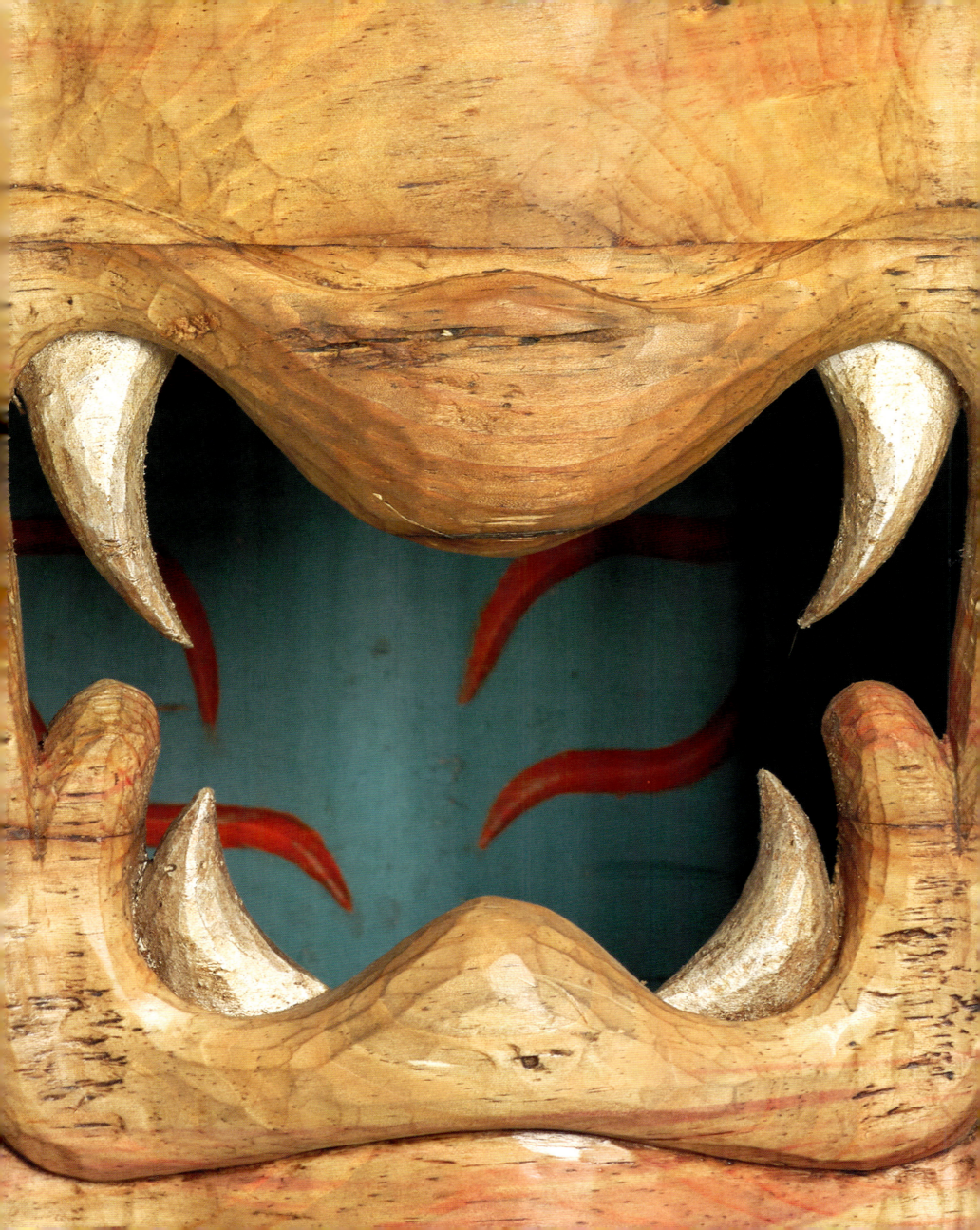

JANE HALLWORTH

Jane Hallworth is an interior designer, a trained architect, and a longtime Blackman Cruz client and collaborator. Her formidable sense of space, color, drama, and savvy curatorial eye make her a favorite among Los Angeles's upper echelons of creative talent.

As an artisan, Hallworth draws on her English upbringing and a passion for architecture, storytelling, and moody themes. But her dramatic narratives never feel dark or crowded. Rather, she reaches toward eccentric, playful symbolism.

Her American Gothic line references Herman Melville's *Moby Dick*, where Captain Ahab's whaling ship *Pequod* is reimagined into a series of industrial, nautical-themed lighting forged in steel. The promise of futurism, space, and dreams define her Odyssey line, where perforations in patinated brass illuminate a feeling of space exploration, and her Constellation lights explore a fascination with mythology and the mystery of the stars.

For Hallworth, lighting is not just a functional necessity; it's a poetic expression as important as any piece of art.

THIERRY JEANNOT

Over ten years ago, artist and designer Thierry Jeannot noticed the clear plastic bottles piling up in front of his studio in the bustling downtown Mexico City neighborhood. He also observed the pepenadores, the people who make a meager living collecting and selling this waste.

Intrigued by the materiality of the plastic, he wondered if he could make chandeliers by using the bottles like glass and include the men and women who collected the raw material as part of the process. He'd never made a chandelier, but he took a risk. He hired the pepenadores, taught them how to hand-cut, dye, and construct thousands of pieces of plastic into dramatic lighting fixtures, reminiscent of classic baroque styles from the sixteenth and seventeenth centuries. The experiment worked. A form once associated with precious crystal became a surprising narrative in which those who once lived on the margins are now part of the process of transforming trash into a luxurious treasure.

Jeannot has added other styles to the collection, like a Sputnik pendant and art deco–inspired wall sconces made from plastic bottlenecks. The formality of decoration mixed with assemblage of cast-off materials has earned Jeannot recognition in the world of decoration and fine art. He has exhibited in museums in Europe, Mexico, and the United States, and has pieces in the permanent collection of Vienna's Museum of Applied Arts and in Paris at Mobilier National.

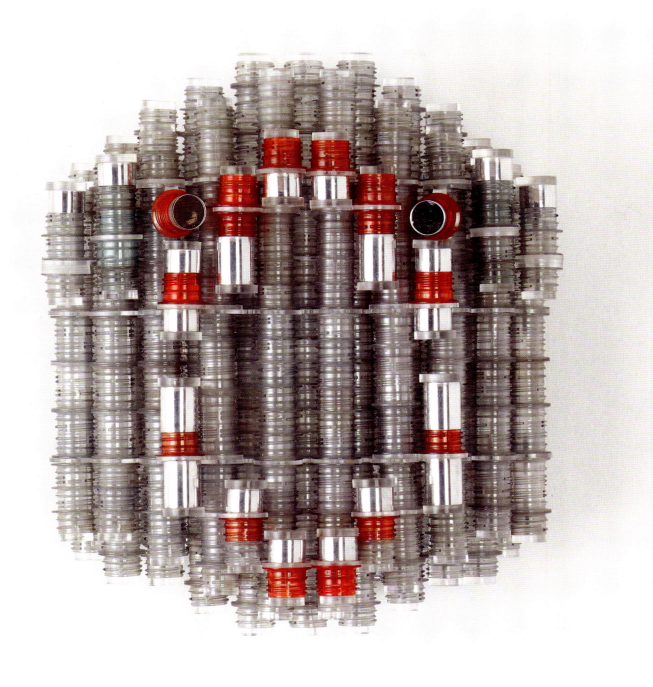

PAGE 267
CLOCKWISE FROM TOP LEFT: *Asnova-Construtto Luminoso* table lamp by Gianni Vallino; *Bakudan Black Resplendor* by Mike Diaz; *Pequod Sconce* by Jane Hallworth; *Templo Mayor* chandelier by Thierry Jeannot

GIANNI VALLINO

PAGE 268
Curva Luminosa Industrial Lamps

PAGE 269
CLOCKWISE FROM LEFT: *Jacques le Fataliste* standing lamps; pair of *Pierre* standing lamps; *Astrolabius* lamp

MIKE DIAZ

PAGE 270
Basalt Xalapa Stool

PAGE 271
TOP TO BOTTOM: *Coimbra Mirror* by Mike Diaz; *Pequod Four Arm Table Lamp* by Jane Hallworth; *Pequod Floor Lamp* by Jane Hallworth; floral installation by Louesa Roebuck; French nineteenth-century sculpting stand; *Tripoli Console* by Mike Diaz; *Sabaudia Daybed* by Mike Diaz

PAGE 272
TOP LEFT: *Noh Table* • TOP RIGHT, LEFT TO RIGHT: Painted and embroidered architectural panel; large amethyst geode specimen; Mike Diaz table lamp • BOTTOM: *Fortezza coffee table*

PAGE 273
Detail of *Noh Table*

JANE HALLWORTH

PAGE 274
Maven hanging fixture

PAGE 275
Phantom Chair

PAGE 276
CLOCKWISE FROM TOP LEFT: *Mariner* light; *Pequod Six Arm Pendant* light; *Stella Sconce*; *Aquila Constellation*

PAGE 277
Detail of *Haunt Pendant*

THIERRY JEANNOT

PAGE 278
Transmutation #14

PAGE 279
Templo Mayor chandelier

PAGE 280
TOP: *Opaline Brass* fixture • BOTTOM: *Morning Star Coffee Table*

PAGE 281
Ikal Sconce

Epilogue

The Blackman Cruz showroom is located in a neighborhood once called the Cahuenga Valley. Like much of Los Angeles, it was an agricultural Shangri-la filled with fragrant citrus and fig groves that disappeared in the early twentieth century after the advent of Hollywood studio lots and housing subdivisions. When Blackman Cruz renovated the property, the architect determined it had been a series of ranch buildings, a remnant from that rural era that had been built up over time. He also discovered the structure's foundation was faulty, even a little dangerous.

Improvements were made, and they brought the building up to code. A reconstruction from something wobbly and precarious into something built to last is a fitting metaphor for how Blackman and Cruz have grown their business over these last thirty years.

Today, the building is resilient, a place where vibrant ideas and dynamic dialogues between people and objects are encouraged. For those, for example, who prefer chairs to people, especially pretty ones that are nice to look at and won't talk back, they can wander the showroom, escaping into an experience that's not much different from visiting a museum or a gallery. There's an algorithm to the Blackman Cruz aesthetic that has the surprising randomness of a John Cage improvisational composition and none of the predictability of a social media scroll. They'll never offer you what they think you want. Instead, they speak their own mind with gestures that defy conventional design rules and preserve craftsmanship from the past so it can be enjoyed in the future.

Approaching decorative arts with such eclectic wonder enables visitors to find joy in the mystery of what's left to discover. Blackman and Cruz will tell you that personal style is not an exact science—that it doesn't have to be elitist or luxurious. They'll say there's hope in that philosophy—that treasures can be yours when you embrace the courage of your convictions so you can recognize what you love when you see it.

Afterword

Working on this book has allowed me a chance to reminisce about the thirty-year journey we've had as furniture and design merchants in Los Angeles. The clients, friends, artisans, employees, and the items we've encountered are woven into the fabric of Blackman Cruz's history. And then there are the highlights . . .

Having an afternoon drink and sit-down with Gore Vidal, enjoying a smoke with Joni Mitchell, being photographed by Annie Leibovitz, having an afternoon hang with David Copperfield at his Vegas home, or being serenaded by Flea at the store's upright piano are just a few of the memorable moments that come to mind.

But besides the memories, I know we've made some solid choices over the years: buying independently from one another, giving a young Lika Moore her start, acquiring our building, and always following our own hearts and vision. As anyone who's been to our showroom knows, we don't follow trends, nor do we conform.

It is the pursuit of that "great thing" that never seems to get old. What's exciting is that every new object opens new worlds. And that's the fun: looking and finding something you never knew existed before this moment in time. And voilà, here it is. This is what keeps us in the game. I guess we're still the same two dealers that first hung out a shingle on La Cienega Boulevard all those years ago. We're still excited by the joy of the hunt.

I know that an afterword is about tying a story up with a neat bow. But our story continues. There's always another great thing out there to find.

—Adam Blackman

Visually encapsulating the thirty-year run of Blackman Cruz is an exercise that is intrinsically flawed—as it is trying to convey it in words. But then again, what isn't?

BC's first incarnation on the corner of La Cienega and Waring had great windows facing the street. Through them we were able to make statements on design, aesthetics, and current affairs. We lovingly ridiculed Los Angeles' obsession with youth, the Oscars' extravagant pageantry, and debates on political correctness. Those windows set the tone of Blackman Cruz and attracted a simpatico clientele, many of whom remain loyal clients and friends.

Early on in our partnership, Adam and I became aware of how we could individually contribute to BC, and we stayed out of each other's way. Luckily, the chemistry worked. Lika, with her reserved, wise ways, added a perfect balance to the stew.

Part of the reason for BC's longevity is the fun we had right from the beginning, and we continue to try to milk fun out of the joint. Our boozy Friday-night speakeasy soirees on La Cienega were a great gateway to the weekend. There were so many characters that eventually became part of the BC scene—old Inge, a Holocaust survivor that Adam befriended who paid us daily visits. She sat in the back and made hysterically funny disparaging remarks about the clientele. Our sales assistant, Shana Blake Hill, surprised us with an operatic farewell performance that filled the place with wondrous sound. Our handyman, Dean, was a three-time award-winning ex–porno star. He worked in the parking lot, barely clad in white T-shirts, causing certain clients to unnecessarily circle the block. And so it went at La Cienega, till the landlady's berserk rent increases compelled us to take the leap and purchase the building that housed Probe, the infamous gay disco on Highland Avenue.

Before taking residence in the space, a cleansing ceremony was performed by my shaman friend, Maria, who provided drums and rattles for everyone. Amy brought the cannabis. We proceeded to rid the place of negativity while leaving the fun vibes. The original dance floor remains, as well as the paneling in the VIP rooms.

We are proud to represent daring and talented designers, and we are always searching for new ones. A great deal of care goes into what we choose to display in the gallery—be it a Carlo Bugatti pedestal commissioned by his friend Marchesa Casati, an Arnaldo Pomodoro bronze plaque, or a manhole cover from Paramount Studios parking lot, the important ingredient is that they deliver a jolt in the belly.

As my mother always said, "Look for the good things, because the bad things will find you regardless." The looking goes on.

—David Cruz

Thank You & Gracias

OUR SPOUSES
We are fortunate to have you by our sides.
Kate Blackman, Richard Hochberg

OUR TEAM
Your support, hard work, and dedication is essential and appreciated.
Phillip Taylor, Lika Moore, Jenny Mason, Jose Macias, Paul Richardson, and Wendy Shepherd

FAMILY
Can't live with you but can't live without you.
Sandy Blackman, the Blackman and Moses families, the Cruz family, the Hochberg family, and the Rivinus family

COLLEAGUES AND FRIENDS
Thank you for all the support and inspiration through the years.
Ryan Murphy, Allen Kolkowitz, Mayer Rus, Ken Erwin, Greg Wooten, Ray Azoulay, Gary Chapman, Pat McGann, Edwin Seth-Brown, Don and Todd Schireson, Jean Brown, Rick and Tracy Cortez, Marcello Frabotta, Richard Wright, Richard Umanoff, Annie Kelly, David Hundley, Heather Lee, Tracy Weston, Marci Blaze, Emmanuel Picault, Juan Elías Robledo, Claudia Grajales, Shannon Koss, Olivia Prime, Jose Mesa, Brian Trembley, and Jose Diaz

THE *BEAUTY & MISCHIEF* TEAM
Thank you all for making this document possible.
Stacie Stukin, Jan Hughes, Iain R. Morris, and the staff at CAMERON + COMPANY

THE PHOTOGRAPHERS
Thank you for your unerring eye and making us look good.
Lendon Flanagan, Roger Davies, David Ross, Tim Street-Porter, Sidney Bensimon, Ian Hughes, Michael Amici, Annie Leibovitz, Ross Floyd, Jonn Coolidge, Fabián Martínez, Aaron Pryor, Jesse Stone, Dusan Vuksanovic, Julius Shulman, Yvan Fiend, and Yoandri Hernandez Perez

IN MEMORIAM
Certainly not forgotten.
Paul Fortune, Vincent Jacquard, Francois Catroux, David Salinas, Dean Tarlton, Pat Quinn, Harrison "Jay" Holman, Inge Wolfe, Jeff Price, Matthew Robinson, Peter Loughrey, Vilma Matchette, Walter Butcher, and Mr. Leap

STACIE STUKIN
Would like to thank
Adam Blackman and David Cruz for being serious people who don't take themselves too seriously. Lika Moore for managing it all with style. Leslie Stoker, of Stoker Literary, who guided us from an idea into a book. Ana Elena Mallet for sharing her expertise in twentieth-century Mexican design. Staci Steinberger, at the Los Angeles County Museum of Art, and Laura Ackerman-Shaw of Ackerman Modern for intel about our passion for Pepe Mendoza. Edgar Lópeznavarrete for his infectious enthusiasm and encyclopedic knowledge of Mexican art, architecture, and design. Stephen DeBro for being on my team.

PAGE 283
Neoclassical grand tour bronze of Mercury after Giambologna

PAGE 285
LEFT TO RIGHT: *Italian eighteenth-century Garden of Eden painting on metal; library table, ca. 1945; Blackman Cruz Workshop (BCW) Snake Chair; Mexican seventeenth-century carved limestone archangel; nineteenth-century painting after William Hogarth,* The End of All Things; *Italian nineteenth-century painted wood collection tray; French brain model by Louis Thomas Jérôme Auzoux, ca. 1850; nineteenth-century papier-mâché skeleton*

PAGE 287
Nineteenth-century European carved-wood sphinx

PAGE 288
Folk art dollar bill, ca. 1965

FRONT COVER
Clarke & Reilly Mennonite petticoat upholstered fauteuil chair with live raven

BACK COVER
Blackman Cruz's version of a Flemish still life with BCW pieces and live snakes

Bibliography

BOOKS

Aarons, Slim. *Poolside with Slim Aarons*/Introduction by William Norwich. New York: Abrams. 2007.

Bailly, Christian. *Automata: The Golden Age, 1848–1914*. London: Sotheby's Publications, 1987.

Buckner, Cory. *Crestwood Hills: The Chronicle of a Modern Utopia*. Los Angeles, Angel City Press, 2015.

Exhibition catalogue: Kaplan, Wendy, ed., *Found in Translation: Design in California and Mexico, 1915–1985*. Los Angeles, California: Los Angeles County Museum of Art; Munich, Germany: New York, NY: Delmonica Books/Prestel, 2017.

Exhibition catalogue: Ryan, Zoë, ed., In a Cloud, *In a Wall, In a chair: Six Modernists in Mexico at Midcentury*. New Haven and London: The Art Institute of Chicago and Yale University Press, 2019.

Faderman, Lillian and Stuart Timmons. *Gay L.A.: A History of Sexual Outlaws, Power Politics, and Lipstick Lesbians*. Basic Books, 2006.

Fortune, Paul. *Notes on Decor, Etc.* New York, Rizzoli, 2018.

Gebhard, David and Harriette Von Breton. *Los Angeles in the Thirties: 1931–1941*. Los Angeles: Hennessey & Ingalls, Inc. 1975, 1989.

Hines, Thomas. *Architecture of the Sun: Los Angeles Modernism 1900–1970*. New York, Rizzoli, 2010.

Miescher, Stephan F. *Gender, Imperialism and Global Exchanges.* John Wiley & Sons, 2015.

Rolle, Elisa. *Queer Places: South and Central America: Retracing the Steps of LGBTQ People Around the World*. San Francisco, Blurb, Inc., 2022.

Shipway, Verna Cook and Warren Shipway. *Mexican Homes of Today*. New York: Architectural Book Publishing Co., Inc. 1964.

Shipway, Verna Cook and Warren Shipway. *Mexican Interiors*. New York: Architectural Book Publishing Co., Inc. 1962.

NEWSPAPERS, MAGAZINES AND JOURNALS

"Decoracion Interior de la Casa Numero 456 del Paseo de la Reforma." *Arquitectura y Decoracion*, October 1937.

Hall Kaplan, Sam. "At the Heights of Mediterranean Style." *Los Angeles Times*, May 21, 1988.

"Hardware from Mexico: José Mendoza." *Interior Design*, June 1957.

Hay, David. "A. Quincy Jones, overlooked genius? Hammer Museum makes the case." *Los Angeles Times*, May 17, 2013.

McCoy, Esther. "Architecture in Mexico." *Arts & Architecture*, August 1951.

"Mexico: Interiors, Decorative Arts, Buying Guide." *Interiors*, December 1963.

Monsiváis, Carlos. "Gays in Mexico: the foundation, expansion, consolidation of the ghetto" *Debate Feminista*, Vol. 26, pp. 89–115, October 2002.

"Paul László: Rich Man's Architect." *Time Magazine*, August 18, 1952.

INTERNET SOURCES

Before the 101: "Paul László's Schiff House," by Kathleen Perricone, date unknown

Hollywood Media District: History, date and author unknown

Queer Maps: Place, probe; unknown date, unknown author

UCLA Library: Center for Oral History Research, "Interview of Paul László: Designing With Spirit," by Marlene Laskey, September, 1985

Whitley Heights Civic Association

INTERVIEWS

Mike Diaz, Blackman Cruz Represented Artist; Mariana Ávila Flynn, Mexico City and New York, Historic Preservation Architect; Jane Hallworth, Hallworth Design and Blackman Cruz represented artist; Thierry Jeannot, Blackman Cruz represented artist; Allen Kolkowitz, Kolkowitz Kusske Architecture; Ana Elena Mallet, Distinguished Professor, Tecnológico de Monterrey, Mexico and independent Mexican design historian and curator; Kathleen Perricone, writer *Before the 101* blog; Laura Ackerman-Shaw, Executive Director, Ackerman Modern; Staci Steinberger, Associate Curator, Decorative Arts and Design, Los Angeles County Museum of Art; Gianna Vallino, Blackman Cruz Represented Artist

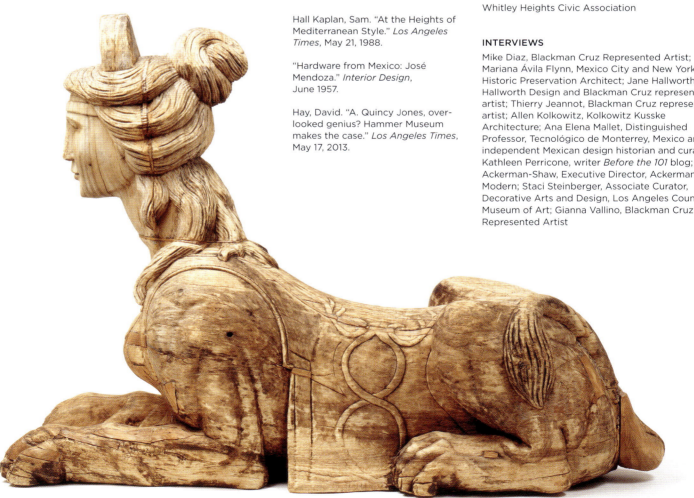

Colophon

CAMERON + COMPANY
Petaluma, California
www.cameronbooks.com

PUBLISHER: Chris Gruener
CREATIVE DIRECTOR & DESIGNER: Iain R. Morris
MANAGING EDITOR: Jan Hughes
MANAGING EDITORIAL ASSISTANT: Krista Keplinger

TEXT COPYRIGHT © 2023 by Blackman Cruz
FOREWORD COPYRIGHT © 2023 by Ryan Murphy
PHOTOGRAPHS © 2022 by Blackman Cruz,
unless otherwise noted

PHOTO CREDITS: Michael D. Amici: 221, 222, 223 • Sidney Bensimon: 13 (*top*), 20–21, 22, 72 (*top*), 84–85 • Adam Blackman: 130 (*top*) • Sandra Blackman: 14 (*top left, top right*) • Jonn Coolidge: 237 (*top right*), 245, 252 (*top*), 253 • David Cruz: 80 (*top*) • Roger Davies: 130 (*bottom*), 143, 148, 149, 177 (*top right, bottom left*), 179, 180, 181, 182–183, 184, 185, 186, 187, 188, 189, 191, 192–193, 194, 195, 196, 197, 198, 199, 202 (*bottom*), 203 (*bottom*), 207 (*top right, bottom left*), 210 (*top right, bottom*) • Yvan Fiend: 279 • Lendon Flanagan: Front and back cover, inside back end paper, 1, 2–3, 11, 12, 13 (*bottom*), 14 (*bottom right*), 15, 16, 17, 30, 31, 32, 33, 38, 39, 40–41, 43, 45, 50, 52, 58 (*top right*), 60–61, 63, 64, 65, 66, 67, 68, 73, 74, 75, 77, 80 (*bottom*), 86, 87, 92, 96–97, 98, 100, 106, 113, 118–119, 123, 126–127, 129, 132, 134, 135, 136, 137, 152–153, 154, 155, 157, 160, 161, 163, 164, 201, 206, 210 (*top left*), 211, 228–229, 230, 232, 233, 234–235, 239 (*top*), 240, 241, 242–243, 246, 251, 254, 256, 287 • Ross Floyd: 4–5, 121, 237 (*bottom right*), 238, 252 (*bottom*), 262 • Courtesy of Hallworth Design: 276 (*top left, bottom*), 277 • Ian Hughes: 44, 56–57, 58 (*top left, bottom left*), 88, 162, 167, 236 (*bottom*), 272 (*top right*) • Annie Leibovitz/Trunk Archive: 10 • Fabián Martínez: 177 (*top left, bottom right*), 212, 213, 214, 215, 216, 217, 218–219, 220 • Yoandri Hernandez Perez: 280 (*bottom*) • Aaron Pryor: 18–19 • David Ross: Spine, front end papers, 24–25, 37, 42, 58 (*bottom right*), 59, 62, 70–71, 72 (*bottom*), 76, 90, 103 (*top*), 110–111, 114, 131, 133, 138–139, 140–141, 158, 159, 165, 170, 171, 174–175, 224–225, 227, 231, 236 (*top*), 237 (*top left, bottom left*), 239 (*bottom*), 244, 247, 248, 249, 250, 255, 257, 258, 259, 264–265, 267, 268, 269, 270, 271, 272 (*top left, bottom*), 273, 274, 275, 276 (*top right*), 278, 280 (*top*), 281 • Julius Schulman © J. Paul Getty Trust. Getty Research Institute, Los Angeles (2004.R.10): 202 (*top*), 203 (*top*) • Jesse Stone: 9 • Tim Street-Porter: 204, 205, 207 (*top left, bottom right*), 208, 209 • Dusan Vuksanovic: 27, 81 • Courtesy of Wright: Inside front end paper, back end papers, 28, 29, 34–35, 36, 46–47, 48–49, 51, 53, 54–55, 69, 78–79, 82, 83, 89, 91 (*right*), 94, 95, 99 (*top right, bottom right*), 101, 102, 103 (*bottom*), 104–105, 107, 108–109, 124–125, 144–145, 146, 147, 151, 156, 168, 169, 172, 260, 261, 283, 285, 288

Published in 2023 by CAMERON + COMPANY, an imprint of ABRAMS.

All rights reserved. No portion of this book may be reproduced, stored in a retrieval system, or transmitted in any form or by any means, mechanical, electronic, photocopying, recording, or otherwise, without written permission from the publisher.

All efforts have been made to locate the contributors and to credit them with the appropriate copyright information. Requests for changes will be considered by the publisher, and any necessary corrections or revisions will be amended in future reprints.

Library of Congress Cataloging-in-Publication Data available.

ISBN: 978-1-951836-97-9

10 9 8 7 6 5 4 3 2 1

Printed in China